T0131659

Haystack Rock

As I approach Haystack Rock my perspective changes. *Every time! My* perspective of life, of God and me… The size of Haystack Rock is hard to fully embrace until you walk in front of it.[1] I was on the south side, walking north along the beach when I first notice a "little" opening, like a doorway into the bottom of this huge rock.

This was a life-changing visual of how God protects me.

> I love you, LORD, my strength. The LORD is my rock, my fortress, and my deliverer; my God is my rock, in whom I take refuge, my shield and the horn of my salvation, my stronghold…. He brought me out into a spacious place; he rescued me because he delighted in me. (Psalm 18:1, 2, 19)

These words remind me every day how strong and precious God is, and how he protects me, because *he delights in me.* Yes, every day I look at the picture on my wall of this huge rock and delightful sky over the ocean. And I am reminded, *again.*

Visits to Haystack Rock have blessed me with *many* life-changing encounters with our Creator, our good Shepherd. I have journaled multiple visuals, messages and confirmations God has given me regarding the new pastures into which he led me. Every visit to Haystack Rock enriches and deepens my relationship with my precious Lord Jesus Christ, my Shepherd.

Hopefully, this memoir will also enhance your encounter with our Shepherd, our Rock.

---

[1] **Haystack Rock** is a 235 ft-tall (72 m) sea stack in Cannon Beach, Oregon. It is the third tallest such intertidal structure in the world. A popular tourist destination on the Oregon Coast, the monolithic rock is adjacent to the beach and accessible by foot at low tide. https://en.wikipedia.org/wiki/Haystack_Rock

I Took You

THE
MAKING OF
A SHEPHERD

God took a less-than-ordinary person on an extra-ordinary journey

Becoming God's Dearly Loved

A Memoir

BEV HISLOP

WESTBOW
PRESS®
A DIVISION OF THOMAS NELSON
& ZONDERVAN

WestBow Press books may be ordered through booksellers or by contacting:

WestBow Press
A Division of Thomas Nelson & Zondervan
1663 Liberty Drive
Bloomington, IN 47403
www.westbowpress.com
844-714-3454

ISBN: 978-1-6642-8983-3 (sc)
ISBN: 978-1-6642-8982-6 (hc)
ISBN: 978-1-6642-8984-0 (e)

Library of Congress Control Number: 2023900999

Print information available on the last page.

WestBow Press rev. date: 02/07/2023

CONTENTS

Setting the Stage

—

I TOOK YOU

The Making of a Shepherd

—

Ordinary me -- Peeking Through the Cracks

Many of us wonder why we are not like others we see through the cracks of our lives. Often, we feel, well ... *just ordinary.*

This memoir tells the story of a person who felt less-than-ordinary most of her life. Yet in mid-life she discovered lies she believed about herself and the unbelievable impact of embracing the truths of being God's dearly loved.

Yes, there is a lot I am still learning about life, about relationships, and about God. But I understand and value more my precious relationship with God, even when it is not pretty or perfect, it is real. Your story is what you have and will always---who you are and who you want to become. You have a choice.

A powerful realization for me was that God could use any and everything in our lives to grow us. *Yes, even someone who feels ordinary.* My prayer is that I will more fully embrace every moment of the life God has given me, for good—for eternal impact.

Will you join me in this?

You are the reason I chose to share this part of my story.

Preface

God gave these two verses to me late in life.

I realized they outline my life
story from the beginning.

I wish I had understood them earlier in life.

But I did not.

—

TAKEN

I took you from the ends of the earth,
from its farthest corners

I called you. I said, 'You are my servant.'

CHOSEN

I have chosen you and have not rejected you.

BROKEN

So do not fear, for I am with you

Do not be dismayed, for I am your God.

GIVEN

I will strengthen you and help you.

I will uphold you with my righteous right hand."

Isaiah 41:9-10

Introduction

"We have gathered today to honor our esteemed colleague."

"In recognition of your twenty years of faithful service at Western Seminary we present this token of our heartfelt appreciation for your ministry of teaching, pastoral care to women and contributing to the academic and personal development of a generation of students who will forever be in your debt as their teacher, mentor, and friend.

Peter exhorted the elders of the church to

"Shepherd the flock of God among you"

(I Peter 5:2) NASB

You have graciously fulfilled this ministry and have modeled the shepherding gift for your students at Western Seminary.

With love and gratitude,

Your Faculty Colleagues.

Dr. Beverly Hislop, Professor of Pastoral Care to Women"

Would you please come forward
to receive your award?

—

Who? That is my name. *What?* Am I dreaming? I must be.

How could I ever get here? I never ever imagined this.

Ordinary me? Cannot be!

A famer's daughter? No way.

My family moved from the Indiana farm to ten acres in the country of central Florida. My DNA said fingers in the dirt, always. Loved it. That is until a poisonous snake showed up. I learned to chop snakes when they visited, and then ask what kind. All while attending grades one through twelve in a small public school in the country.

Life in town was an unknown. People looked at me funny. I did not realize at the time that I was poor, and I dressed that way. An introvert rarely steps forward to speak. She gathers and stores away inherent messages from others.

You are not enough.

You are worthless, despicable, ugly, unlovable.

You must meet our expectations.

We don't want you. In fact, we would be better off without you!

I believed all of these.

"Bev, stay on the couch. Don't cause work for us. Be quiet."

I never had a choice.

Or did I?

Popularity. Performance. Possessions.

I tried to change people's perspective of me, to meet their expectations.

Exhausted and defeated. It did not work.

Back on the couch.

From that couch I wondered what life was like "out there," outside my small world. I began *peeking through the cracks.*

Being God's Dearly Loved

Being God's dearly loved means letting the truth of our *being dearly loved* become enfleshed in everything we think, say, or do. It typically comes in four phases.

1. Taken 2. Chosen. 3. Broken. 4. Given

—

1. TAKEN

"**I took you** from the ends of the earth,
from its farthest corners

I called you. I said, 'You are my
servant'." (Isaiah 41:9)

Not me!

I do not feel "taken" by God.

How could I be "called" by God?

He would not pick me.

I am not good enough. I *feel* rejected.

Chapter 1

The Cracks

There is little memory of those early years, with one exception.

I was six years old and wished for new friends in the Hialeah, Florida trailer park. There was a young girl close to my age who came over to swing with me. We played as six-year-olds do—laughing, jumping, and swinging together.

One day she asked, "Would you like to go shopping with me and my mom tomorrow?"

"Really? Yes!"

I was elated! I had never "gone shopping." It seemed like an adult thing to do. I could not believe she was asking *me*. I was elated. *Did I already say that?*

I hardly slept. I picked out my best dress and found a little purse to take. I thought, *I look grown up, don't I?* Disney World did not exist back then, at least not the one we know about today. But today I would say that best describes how I felt. Like I was going to Disney World with my new friend. A beyond-description-excitement.

I got dressed. Then waited and waited.

There she was.

Her mom was driving, and my new friend was in the front

passenger's seat. They pulled up to our trailer. I ran outside and hurried to the car as my friend rolled down the window and shouted, "You can't go with us. We don't want you."

She quickly rolled up the window. They drove off. I never saw her again.

She does not want me? She does not want me. Her mother does not want me. *Does anyone want me?*

Little did I know how deeply those words would invade my life.

The cracks in my life began to open.

—

The cracks between the rotting wooden planks let in a small streak of light. The gnats and roaches followed. Wrinkled, soiled sheets reaching the sandy floor filled the narrow spaces.

"Bob, it's your brother Ray. I'm here from Florida to see you."

Uncle Bob's eyes opened, and a weak smile surfaced for a second or two. My dad held Uncle Bob's thinning arm and hand. "How are you?"

My mom looked on.

As Mom and Dad entered the room, Nellie stepped outside, lack of space. Nellie had brought Uncle Bob this far and was staying until the end. She was Uncle Bob's mate. My brothers and I could only peek through the cracks of Uncle Bob's one-room house.

Mississippi was a new place for me. So was Uncle Bob—a new relative to me. I did not remember ever seeing him before. I knew he had served in a war. I did not realize war left men like Uncle Bob so torn up.

My dad began singing, "When the roll is called up yonder, I'll be there." Uncle Bob likely thought he was in heaven. He opened his mouth a bit, mostly drool. A dry sound eked out now and then.

Uncle Bob slept most of the time, too weak to get up. Nellie found food somewhere. Bob drank when Nellie put a cup to his mouth. I do not know where she slept. There was just a pile of pillows in the corner.

"Is this what war is like, Dad?"

"Sometimes."

"Did *you* want to go to war *too*?"

"I wanted to serve my country in the military."

"Why didn't you?"

"They disqualified me because I had rheumatic fever as a child, which gave me an enlarged heart."

"But didn't Uncle Wilbur die in the war?"

"Yes, in Europe during World War II. My brother Bob served in the Korean War."

"How did Uncle Eugene die?"

"He had a disease some of my family inherited. My mother,

Uncle Eugene, his two daughters, and a sister all died of what is called Huntington's chorea disease.1 They have no cure for it."

Will I die of it? My twelve-year-old mind struggled to understand.

———

A year later I traveled to Indiana with my family for my fifteen-year-old cousin Patty's funeral. It was shocking, Huntington's chorea disease. *How could she be only two years older than me, yet die? How could someone that young die from a cause she had no control over or power to eradicate?*

Will I die of it? The thought resurfaced again.

Huntington's chorea disease had killed Patty's seventeen-year-old sister Barb two years earlier. We did not go to the funeral. It still seemed unreal.

What if this was all I *got to live on the earth – thirteen years?*

None of us knew. It was not a choice. Why did *they* get the hereditary disease? Their dad had it and died from it. We were told if a parent had it, there was fifty percent chance each child would get it. *Would I be exempt? Or not?* It was an on-going question I lived with but tried to stuff when it surfaced. Because no one was talking about it, I assumed it was inappropriate to raise the question. So, I did not.

I internalized my own weakness and powerlessness to forge a predictable life.

———

I often looked back on those earlier years.

My dad's dear father, Clarence, outlived six of his seven adult children and his wife. The hereditary disease, plus military service in the wars were the main culprits.

It seemed within minutes being in Grampa's company, a Bible verse would easily flow from his lips. It obviously came from deep within his heart, as each painful death or disease threatened to overcome his love for family and God. Yet, as biblical Job wrestled with his losses, so did Grampa. Job, realizing he did not know God as well as he first thought, grew in his relationship with God through the pain. "My ears had heard of you but now my eyes have seen you." (Job 42:5)

Job refocused. So did Grampa. He would say, "God is good. God loves me. God is always present to strengthen me amid the pain. He is and he does." Grampa, his siblings, and his children farmed extensive acreage surrounding and beyond Bass Lake in Knox, Indiana. Life in this farming community must go on.

And it did.

My dad had rheumatic fever as a child. It was not until he and the family physically fought a wildfire threatening the farm, that they recognized his heart was different.

Life in the farming community continued. On weekends, Dad drove us from our home in South Bend, Indiana to Knox. Dad was building a small house for us, next to his relatives on the family farm. It was a slow build. Cold weekends left my five-year-old body wanting to stand on the heat vent in our current house, not get in a cold car for the one-hour drive to the family farm.

Yet Dad's brothers-in-law, sisters, uncles, aunts, and of course Grampa welcomed us each weekend and helped Dad with building. Week after week, month after month, I felt more at home on the farm. My joy increased each time we were there. We looked forward to becoming full-time farmers. I felt like a farmer's daughter.

Mom gave birth prematurely to our third sibling, Palmer. Understandably, he took most of her focus. My brother Paul and I shared good times at home. We built snowmen. We ate the exceptionally long icicles hanging from the house roof down to the snow-covered ground. In summer we played under the huge willow shade tree. Eventually little Palmer joined us, lying outside on a blanket with his toys. We rode tricycles and played with our neighborhood friends.

And then…

Paul developed bronchitis. The medical doctor tried all he knew to do. Eventually he told my parents that they had only one option. "You need to move your family to a warmer climate."

What? Move from Indiana? *Now?* Give up snow, icicles? Give up the vision of farming? Leave this family farm?

My parents struggled. They prayed. They talked. They prayed more. Time passed.

Dad had an older brother. Uncle Alvin lived in Apopka, Florida.

What would Dad do for a job? He was working as a bookkeeper at Bendix in South Bend.

Dad and Mom talked more. And yes, prayed more.

Eventually Dad got a job in finances at a packing company in Hialeah, Florida. How far away was that? A four-hour drive from Uncle Alvin. A twenty-plus hour drive from South Bend—*from home.*

Dad drove all five of us, very closely seated in our small car, to Hialeah from Indiana. Dad and Mom purchased a one-bedroom trailer and parked it in a neighborhood trailer park. My two brothers and I slept on the fold-out couch. It was not long before my mom came home from the hospital with our baby sister, Carole. Dad squeezed a tiny crib into the bedroom next to their bed.

We spent most of the day outside on a swing set and teeter-totter with other kids. We enjoyed the south Florida sunshine, the warmth, and the space outside.

Until *that* girl.

And the cracks opened.

Chapter 2

The Next Queen of New Zealand

We left Hialeah when my dad found a job as comptroller at Correct Craft Boat Company near Orlando. He purchased ten acres in rural Apopka. We lived in the same trailer we had in Hialeah, now back in the wooded area of the lot. My dad was building a house on the front of the property.

One day my brother and I snuck up the hill to our neighbor's house. I was nearly eight, my brother six. The walls of worn wooden slats were rough but gave us a few cracks to peek inside. The wood rotting on the porch kept us from stepping up for a closer look.

We had heard from another neighbor that the next queen of New Zealand lived here. We wanted to see her. She must be beautiful. We wondered, *where is New Zealand?* It did not matter. She was the next queen.

We tried to look in a window. We did not see a throne or any sign of a crown. Not even high heels. Nothing golden.

"Hey, ya wanna play ball?" A boy and girl ran out to meet us. They lived there.

"Can we come in?"

"No. We have to play outside." *We don't want you* sounded in my head again.

We played often. *Always* outside their house. We *always*

wished we could see the queen. We asked each time we played. They simply said, "No. We have to play outside." Those words always sounded like, *we don't want you.*

We became used to the scenario. My mom was able to talk to her, but we were not. We never saw her. Sometimes Mom brought her cookies. I guess that is what you do for a future queen.

The few times we saw their dad getting out of his car, he was friendly to us. He worked at a blueprint shop in town. A great surprise came the one day he asked his daughter and me if we wanted to visit his shop. We did. It was the first time I ever had a Coke—and it came out of a machine after he put in some coins. What a fun game to play. I guess that is what royalty gets to do *every day.*

We never got inside to see the next queen. Only Mom did.

Years later I learned that my mom often took food to her, to help the family survive. Empty alcohol bottles, no heat, and facial scars were all clues my mom did not miss. I was too young to see, too young to understand. But Mom did. My mom cared about people. She understood family pain.

———

My dad left early for work each weekday to drive the forty-five-plus minutes from Apopka into Pine Castle, south of Orlando. When he was home, he would build our three-bedroom cement block house on the front of our ten acres. Once the foundation was laid, we played on the concrete floors with tricycle, wagon, and games. Once the studs were installed, we could make up new games to play from room to room. We loved the new inside playground.

I can still picture Dad atop the roof as he stapled down each new shingle. He was strong and a hard worker. His creativity showed up often. He shoveled a good-sized hole in the backyard, then laid a canvas into it before filling it with water. Then he announced the gift of our own "swimming pool!" We felt privileged.

A warm outside led us to build playhouses out of palmetto branches. We also made tree houses, and we talked to each other from tree to tree through a tin can attached by a hose. Orange groves were across the street. We tasted one or two.

Mom would build an outdoor wood fire so she could heat water in a huge cast iron pot. She poured the warm water into a wringer-type washing machine sitting on the house's open concrete foundation. She worked extremely hard to simply keep her four children in clean used clothes. When she was able to get fabric, she would sew an outfit for us, or repair used ones. One of my favorite coats was made from two worn-out adult coats, cut and restyled. It was thick and warm, unlike most children's coats. I felt like an adult wearing it.

Food was scarce. At the end of the week, we could count on having soup, made from leftovers. We never knew what would be in it. At the time I could hardly swallow it. Just the thoughts of "used food" made me want to gag. Years later when I tried to use "leftovers," I began to appreciate the amazing flavors Mom had created with so little.

Our mom was a queen in her own right. She deserved the crown, the throne, and the high heels. My eight-year-old eyes could not see it. At that point, her story was still being written. And so was mine. Years later, I would see.

Those early years were filled with not wanting to add more work to my mom's day. I was the oldest. I could take care of myself. She had my three younger siblings who needed her constant care. I chose to sit outside on the swing or play in the woods. Be quiet. Be invisible.

Or go up the hill and look for the next queen of New Zealand.

Chapter 3

A Start Over

It felt like a new life. A start over.

First grade.

I liked my teacher, Miss Brown. We were all new at this small country Apopka Elementary School. No kindergarten back then.

Each day after lunch Miss Brown had us take a break, a quiet time lying on a towel or blanket we brought from home. Mary (not her real name) was next to me and friendly. One day our quiet conversation led us to focus on a photo posted on the bulletin board above us. We could not tell if the rabbit was smiling or hungry. Mary prompted me to get up and get the picture. She wanted a closer look. I wanted a friend. The thumb tacks were tighter than I imagined. After removing one, I worked on the second one. It took both hands.

Suddenly the first thumb tack, held in my lips, started down my throat. I started choking. Mary gave me water to drink. More water. Choking lessoned, slowly. Eventually it went down. Down, *then where?*

Next thing I knew, I was on the way to the doctor. Fortunately, the tack was upside down. Punctures were avoided. He gave me a special diet to hopefully encourage the tack to continue its journey all the way into the toilet.

It did, eventually.

And I saw Mary as my new friend.

—

A bigger surprise came when my first-grade class voted me to represent them in the May Day King and Queen Court. I was shocked. *Me?*

My classmates noticed me? Liked me? Wanted me? How could this be?

I dressed up in a special yellow dress my mom made. I marched with Roger and sat next to him on the lowest level in the high stadium. The sixth-grade king and queen sat at the top. She wore the crown and had high heels.

It felt like a great honor, a whole new experience.

I did not have a model's smile. I did not know I should. Pictures revealed I was simply absorbing all that was happening in front of the court. Students from every grade were performing. And I was watching.

Was I dreaming? Pictures confirmed someone wanted me.

In first grade.

—

Each birthday I received a birthday card all the way from Knox, Indiana. It was addressed to "Beverly." It felt special. Inside were a couple of dollars and a verse from the Bible.

Grampa wrote it in his own handwriting. It ended with "Love, Grampa."

In a world with almost no verbal expressions of love, this meant everything to a little girl living on ten acres out in the country.

—

I started third grade feeling surprisingly good about life.

It was "over the top" to have an invitation to an overnight birthday party from the most popular girl in school, Linda (not her real name). This was a *big deal*. I could not believe I got invited. Her family was rich, they owned a store in town. There was lots of food and music. Since I was the only one who did not know how to dance, they offered to teach me. It was great fun.

The next morning Linda's mother drove me home. She seemed a bit surprised when she pulled into the dirt driveway that led to a tiny trailer in the woods. I thanked her and she quickly drove away.

The next day at school I could hardly wait to tell Linda how much fun I had. Before I could get the words out, she said, "My mom said I cannot be friends with you. I cannot even talk with you at school. So, I will not. Goodbye."

She never did. I did not understand why.

In my head I heard those words again. *We don't want you. You can't go with us.*

I moved back into my shell and tried to go unnoticed, especially to the popular students.

—

That Christmas my mom's parents came from Indiana to Florida. Grandma told us she wanted to tell her friends back in South Bend that it was warm enough in Florida to go to the beach on Christmas day. Even though Grandpa disagreed with Grandma—as always—he did hop into the station wagon with us and rode to Daytona Beach.

As soon as we arrived, we got out and walked around the car one time. We felt the chilly wind – Grandpa disagreed that it was cold—and then got back into the car and drove home.

As soon as we got home Grandma told me she had a gift for me.

This was a *first*.

Honestly, I was not even sure she knew I existed. Yet was I about to have my uncertainties changed forever? Hope and excitement began to surface.

She came over to me with a closed fist. She opened her hand and there was a pile of small metal circles connected to each other. Once I lifted it up, I realized it was a bracelet.

A bracelet – *just for me?* A first. *I could not believe my eyes.*

As I lifted it out of her hand, I noticed it had a name on it, created by the metal letters: Susan. I looked at it. I looked at Grandma. I looked at it again. *Didn't she know my name?*

It was then she said she found it on the floor of the bus they rode to Florida.

She had not thought about me and wanted to give me something. She had not purchased it just for me. Not even a Christmas present. I was crushed.

Don't anticipate this as joy or fun because you will be disappointed every time.

———

Our family drove from Florida to Indiana most summers for vacation. We spent most of our time visiting Dad's family in Knox. I made a lot of assumptions during those visits. It seemed the only way to navigate being unnoticed was to remain seated on the couch. My younger siblings all went into the playhouse attic with cousins their age. The adults were in deep conversation in the kitchen and outside. No one reached out to include me. I assumed all agreed, *you cannot go with us. We would be better off without you.*

I thought if I did not cause any trouble, was quiet and simply stayed put on that couch, I was filling my role in the family. The *we do not want you* jumped on board and joined the already acclaimed *we would be better off without you,* frequently.

———

It was near the end of the semester in seventh grade. I loved school, learning, and expanding my small world. Advanced classes were motivating. Grades revealed challenging work and discipline. I worked hard to bring valuable contributions to class discussions. Near the end of the semester something my English teacher said was not clear to me. I raised my hand and asked her to clarify.

She called on me. I asked the question.

She gave me a very cold stare. Dead silence. More silence.

My feet shifted.

"Remember at the beginning of the semester I told the class that if any of you ask a stupid question, I will not answer. I will simply be silent. This is a stupid question."

Sweat poured out.

My face felt red.

The message surfaced quickly.

I am not good enough. We want you to meet our expectations.

How could I ever face her and my classmates again? I felt… well, never able to meet their expectations.

———

At the beginning of eighth grade, each homeroom class was asked to vote for our Student Council Representative. It was a given that popular Linda would get elected.

We voted.

Just as the outcome was to be announced, the teacher said Linda and Bev were both "runners up." This called for a second vote. *How could this be? Of course she would win. This would simply press deeper the pain of that reality.*

"Close your eyes everyone. Those voting for Linda, please raise your hands. Keep them up until I count them all. Thank you. Now those voting for Bev, please raise your hands."

The outcome was obvious. The delay in counting Linda's and the pace at which mine were counted ... *it was a given.*

"Students, our next Student Council Representative is .... deep breath.... Beverly. By two votes. Congratulations Bev!"

Immediately the class began chanting, "Speech. Speech. Speech."

How could this be? Did the teacher count correctly? Did my fellow students really want me? I was so shocked. I could not speak. They continued chanting. The teacher turned to me and said, "Say something."

I slowly walked up front. Linda should have won. She loved being up front. She had the look and the words. *Not me, never. I was sweating. I was sure I did not look like I should win. I did not look like a leader, rather a scared bunny rabbit. I wanted to run into the forest as fast as I could and hide.*

All I remember saying is something like, "Thank you. I will do the best I can ..."

I cried when I got home. *How did I even win?* The way I responded to the students' chant to speak confirmed I was not good enough. I was sure I did not meet their expectations. This had to be a mistake ... *They were probably already sorry they voted for me.*

But when I woke up the next morning knowing I had to face my classmates again, I made a vow-of-sorts with myself. I would honestly try to be the best Student Council Representative I possibly could. I took that leadership task very seriously. If my classmates had that much confidence in me, I did not want to disappoint them. Rather, I wanted to go "over the top" in representing them and contributing to the school.

That vow stayed with me through the rest of my high school years, including times when *I'm not good enough* came calling, again, and again.

Yes, a start over.

Chapter 4

Pour Kool-Aid and Wear Nylons

"Bev, what are you going to do after graduation?"

Mr. Hubbard, a local community college professor, taught College Prep English at our high school. He asked me to come up to the front of the classroom to his desk. It was the last day of class. The other students were leaving. This was my last high school class.

"I'm planning to attend Emmaus Bible School in Oak Park, Illinois, for their one-year certificate program," I answered.

He looked at me with surprise. Then caught himself.

"Well, will you promise me this? Whenever you finish with *whatever that is*, you will go to college. *You are college material.*"

No one had ever mentioned college to me. Not my parents. No other teachers. I assumed I had to learn to pour Kool-Aid for little kids ... like all good church women.

I never forgot his words.

They touched a deep place and the desire to go to college lingered.

Am I really college material?

—

I grew up believing that I was "less than" in God's sight. I felt "less than" in the eyes of our church leaders. I wanted to give God my whole heart, my whole life. Yet when I went into the church kitchen where women were supposed to be, I ended up in the corner listening to a woman's painful story. *How did that happen?*

The tradition clearly taught that the only service women could do was "pour Kool-Aid and wipe little noses." Women could serve in the kitchen and make food for everyone, or they could take care of little children during church service. I had neither skill.

Every time I read Jesus's words to Martha, I felt I was more like Mary. Yet, I did not think I was supposed to be sitting at Jesus feet listening, learning. Rather women were to be in the kitchen preparing food, right? "Martha was distracted by all the preparations that had to be made. She came to him and asked, 'Lord, don't you care that my sister has left me to do the work by myself? Tell her to help me!" *Did Jesus?*

"Martha, Martha, the Lord answered, you are worried and upset about many things, but few things are needed—or indeed only one. Mary has chosen what is better and it will not be taken away from her" (Luke 10:38-42). I could not think of another way to interpret this text other than to say, Jesus thought it was okay for a woman to listen, learn, and spend time with him. His words said it was "better" than "all the preparations" in the kitchen. No one else was saying that in my world.

The church weekly communion service was one hour

scheduled before the preaching service. The communion service was designed for words of praise to God—either in song, Scripture reading, prayer, or comments—to be given spontaneously ("Spirit led") with only the planned serving of communion at the end. A great format.

The one restriction was for women. Women had to wear head coverings and could not participate audibly. "Women worship silently, while men worship audibly," we were taught.

—

There were few activities for high schoolers in our church. I was in eleventh grade. I had a fervent desire to plan something, to start something for youth. My desire lingered.

I finally decided I needed to ask the church leadership. *Did I have enough courage?* They were all men. They were kind enough. Yet, I knew it was not acceptable for a woman to ask about leadership.

The ongoing desire was so strong, I took a deep breath. Then asked three high school friends to go with me—my girlfriend and two church guys we be-friended. They agreed. We talked about it and realized we all had similar desires. They were excited about the possibilities.

We asked the elders.

No response.

Days later an elder said they would get back with us *on that.*

When? As time went on, I assured myself they would *never* let us plan something. Again, I was sure they were thinking, *we'd be better off without you, we don't want you.* Perhaps they would find a way to silence us. Get rid of us.

Day after day, week after week went by.

Then I got a phone call. A middle-aged man asked me to bring my friends to the back of the church on Sunday. He had something to tell us. I could hardly breathe. I hung up scared.

We stood ready at the back of the church. He walked slowly toward us. "The elders asked me to lead you. However, I believe you four are a lot more capable than I am to serve youth. I trust you to plan events and carry them out. Simply keep me updated."

Really? Did the elders know he would not be with us every minute of planning or at the events? Or was that simply his decision? Would trouble come later?

"…plan events and carry them out," he said.

So, we did!

We enjoyed being together and worked well as a team. We focused on each other's desires and gifts: Lois, Tom, Joe, and me. We planned weekly events, and eventually a state-wide event. We also attended the weekly Youth for Christ Orlando rallies with students from multiple high schools in the area. What a great gathering of hundreds of teens each week. Incredible encouragement and growth resulted. We experienced our church camp together.

For our state-wide event we rented a conference room upstairs in a local bank. The four of us planned it, yet each had specific areas of follow-through. Lois planned and provided the food. I visualized and implemented essential elements of the program. Tom and Joe provided publicity, staging and clean-up.

Later in life Lois established her own Italian restaurant. Tom's credentials and profession focused on advising towns how to increase tourism. Joe had his own property management business. Those early experiences reflected the skill set of each of us. We enjoyed working together as well. All four of us still treasure those two years working as a *team*—with the full trust of the man chosen to simply oversee us. *Would this ever be possible again in life?* I wished.

—

Months later, I stepped out of the car onto the sidewalk with my suitcases in front of Emmaus Bible School at Oak Park, Illinois. My parents drove me from Florida to my new school. I repeated my parents' words. "Good-bye. See you later."

My parents and siblings simply continued their drive to visit relatives in Indiana. At the time it seemed a normal good-bye for us. There were no hugs, no tears, no emotional words. I knew they loved me and were glad for this choice of schooling. My sister would now have a bedroom all to herself. She was in junior high school. I knew she would be glad.

I thought I was ready for this next chapter in life.

I made my way to Emmaus Bible School's (EBS) front

office, and they told me my dorm room was on the third, the top floor. It became obvious I was a day earlier than most students. So, I simply carried my bags in two trips up the stairs.

I had one roommate who had not arrived yet, so I could use one side of the closet and one dresser. It was a surprise to see a pipe twelve inches above the floor running the length of the room—which meant stepping up over it each time I wanted to get into my bunk. I hoped I would remember it was there in the middle of the night. I did most nights.

On my walk back down the stairs, a woman stopped me. She introduced herself as the Dean of Women. She put her hand on my legs. "You don't have nylons on!"

"No. I don't need them. We have tanned legs in Florida."

She did not seem to understand. "You are required to wear nylons here."

What? Where have I landed? I came here because I knew the Christians in my life would approve. EBS was a school that our church supported.

The words began to settle into my thinking: *we want you to meet our expectations. You are not enough.*

More surprises followed.

Chapter 5

The Guys Sat on the Left Side

The guys sat on the left side in each classroom. The girls sat on the right side, with a wide walkway between. In the EBS library guys and girls could not sit at the same table. In the hallway between classes, guys and girls could not talk to each other. And of course, guys and girls could never be seen holding hands or in any way touching each other. They would be expelled.

Welcome to Emmaus Bible School (EBS), 1965.

I eventually learned there was no inter-racial/international dating. This was beyond comprehension when I heard it applied to my friend—an American girl—who could not date a Canadian guy. *What? Where have I landed?* Eventually they married and served as missionaries in Mexico.

I found the courses intriguing. We studied Bible, theology, and Christian living. I valued the studies. But most of all, I benefitted from the safety of asking one of my professors, Dr. N. Smith, the questions I was hesitant to ask my home church leaders.

Many of these had to do with pouring Kool-Aid and wiping little noses—*or not.* Was that really all that God put me on the planet to do in the church community? If so, why did I not have those skills/gifts or desires?

That narrow pathway began to expand when Dr. Smith took me to the texts that clearly showed spiritual gifts were not gender specific. While local churches decide where certain gifts could be used by women, the Bible did not differentiate in that specific text.

And so, my future world began to slowly open. *God, is there a place for me other than the kitchen or nursery? If so, where?* Although the fear of not meeting expectations surfaced often, safe conversations gave me hope.

—

EBS had a good male basketball team that played other schools. Yet, we had no cheerleaders. Other schools did. *Why didn't we?*

I surprised myself by asking a handful of girls to join me in cheering for our school at the next game. It was fun, energizing, and joyful ... but only lasted until we were told to stop at the second game. *We don't want you.*

Dr. Smith agreed to be the coach for a woman's basketball team. One was formed. I loved playing, short me--I even scored a few points for my team.

Again, that lasted only a few weeks.

Don't anticipate this as joy or fun. You will be disappointed every time.

I did not have money to fly home for Thanksgiving, so was very thankful someone invited me and other students to their home. There were likely twenty-five of us around that long table. I enjoyed the food and tried to listen to all the voices around me. However, I felt invisible. No one talked directly to me. I did not realize it at the time, but I was playing my role of "lost child." *You would be better off without me, so I will play that role for you.*

Christmas break brought the joy of flying home to Florida. I missed home, friends and family that fall semester. Yet, once I finally arrived home, I was surprised to see that I had changed. They had not. I could not define my changes, but I thought differently now than when I had left home.

Oh, my love for the Lord Jesus was stronger. I believed he loved me and wanted me in his family. I did not know the implications of what I was learning about God and myself, yet I wanted to explore them further.

I returned to EBS in Oak Park, Illinois, with a new determination.

—

The Spring term held several unexpected experiences.

The first was receiving word that my dad was going to have open-heart surgery in Cleveland, Ohio in February. Dad's rheumatic fever episode as a young man, left him with an enlarged heart. It was the severe pain of gallstones—requiring surgery—that led doctors to say he would need an artificial heart valve in place before they would consider doing surgery for gallstones. The on-going pain of gallstones intensified my dad's decision.

Doctors said it should be done within the year. Dad was 43 years old.

At the time, artificial heart valve replacement was a new procedure that could only be done in select locations. Cleveland was the closest to Florida, so my parents had little choice. Dad was hospitalized and given multiple tests at the recommendation of his Florida doctors. The extended process was challenging. The outcome confirmed an enlarged heart, leakage of the valves, the mitral valve distorted and obstructed.

I was thankful to be closer geographically to the hospital and have opportunity to see my dad. It was great that my mom, Connie, would be there with Dad the entire time. Mom waited alone through each slow-moving hour. Midafternoon she was given permission to go into ICU and see Dad briefly. He was not awake, but the machines said he was breathing. Three days later I was able to see him. That worked out well since only one person could see Dad for five minutes each day. Mom gave this day to me.

Seeing someone you love in ICU for the first time…. well… I was glad they told me he was in that bed because I could not see him. I reached out to touch his hand. I felt nauseated. I looked down at the bed and wondered. *Where is he?* I could not see his face. It was covered with breathing stuff. Was he alive? I was lightheaded. I felt like I was going to faint. I had never seen anyone in a hospital bed, specifically not in ICU. I did not know what to expect. The last time I saw my dad he spoke to me, he smiled. The shock overwhelmed me. I felt helpless. The nurse led me out of the room. *Was he going to live again?*

I calmed down as I sat with my mom. Mom put her arm around my shoulders. We both felt the emotion of watching and waiting for our loved one to regain consciousness. We teared up when we thought he might not. After a bit of silence, we searched for words we thought would encourage one another. Mom said she prayed every day and, "Lots of people are praying for his recovery. Everyone at church knows. Dad has faith too."

My dad's extensive writing was quite descriptive of the experience from his perspective. One brief quote he wrote *after he was back home*:

> On Monday morning the usual invasion of ten to twenty doctors expressed gratitude at my progress. By now I could perceive the action of the new Teflon and Dacron ball and cage type valve in my heart. Somehow it gave me a new feeling. I was told that I would probably be going upstairs that day. I felt as if this was a real victory.
>
> Connie had been allowed to visit me three brief times and Beverly had come up once on Sunday but had become nauseated and had to leave after a couple of minutes. I was thankful for the short visits; only five-minute periods were allowed. By now "upstairs" meant regular visiting hours.

Connie later told me she also became sick the first day she visited me in Constant Care.

My ride back to school came the next day. It was hard to leave Dad. I hoped I would never see him again in that ICU position, rather life back to normal.

I was glad to hear he returned home to Florida nearly two weeks later. He said he felt chest pain with every breath … for three months and beyond. It was challenging for Dad, to say the least, yet he felt blessed to be alive. We assumed "normal life" would resume. And it seemed to. My dad eventually went back to his comptroller job at Correct Craft Boat Company in Orlando. His health was greatly improved.

—

My focus on school increased.

This was my last semester and that intensified my desire to gain all I could. Increased wisdom expanded understanding of my faith and time with friends.

I got a job at the local public library, which was a short walk across the park from the school. I had good co-workers and supervisors—both men and women. They both provided positive input along the way. It was great to feel I contributed to a valuable cause. It was a new experience to work in such an environment.

The biggest surprise came when the librarians Elizabeth and Lester initiated a "Farewell—Thank You" surprise for me with all twenty-seven employees signing the good-bye card at the end of the school year.

What happened to the belief I had embraced my whole life? Don't anticipate this as joy or fun. You will be disappointed every time.

Was this just a lie I had believed? Could this *joy* really be happening *to me?*

—

On one of those days as I walked across the park returning from my job, a friend sitting on a park bench stopped me. He was a student who often sang and played guitar at school events.

I sat down.

"How are you doing today, Bev?"

"Good. It was another good day at the library."

"Great. There is something I wanted to ask you."

"Sure. What?"

"Bev, God told me to ask you to marry me. *Will you?*"

What? I liked him and his music. But *marry?*

We were at a school that did not believe God speaks to us today, and I had not explored that belief further—yet. *How could he possibly have heard that?*

My response to him was simple and brief. "Well, God has not told me. So perhaps you need to ask God to tell me too."

I do not know if my friend did.

God did not.

The following summer he met a girl at summer camp. They married and still serve as missionaries. Apparently, he simply got the name wrong.

—

As that final semester progressed, I was beginning to question the belief I had carried all my life to that point. *We don't want you. We'd be better off without you.*

It was subconscious at times, but I began to expect that kind of reaction to my presence, or my questions. Even more so in a Christian environment *because I was a woman.* A woman without Kool-Aid or runny nose skills. *Would the guys always sit on the other side of the room from me? Was there really a place for me?*

Professor N. Smith encouraged me to question those deep-seated beliefs. He asked questions that further stimulated my thinking.

What did God think about me? Did God want me? I so wanted to please God, but was not sure how, given the seeming lack of skills required.

I completed the EBS One-Year Biblical Certificate with a sense of accomplishment, alongside a desire for further exploration of what life held for me.

… Not just on the right side of the room.

Chapter 6

Listen to this Piece of Music

"Listen to this piece of music. As it is being played, write it out on the blank sheet music grand staff at your desk."

Were we really to write the actual notes—treble clef, bass clef, including flats and sharps, *and* the timing—while listening *only once* to the music?

Yes.

In my search to find what my role in life would be, I took several music courses at Orlando Junior College after coming back home to Florida from EBS in Illinois. They brought joy and I thought might have long-term potential. That is until I encountered this in-class exercise. The class instructor played the music *only once*.

I went home that day again hearing, *we want you to meet our expectations.*

I could not.

I tried an art class. It was my first. I loved seeing displayed artwork by others. Most students had taken art in high school. Not me. I learned a lot, but the consistent "C" grade said I was only average. Again, I heard, *we want you to meet our expectations.*

Again, I could not.

These were interests of mine but apparently, I did not have significant skills. I completed the school year with a variety of courses, still asking what would be my career? I loved school and hoped to continue—yet what program?

—

Before fall classes started, I looked for a summer job. My love for summer camp surfaced. There was an opening all summer to serve in various roles at Camp Horizon in Orange Springs, Florida.

I applied.

I was accepted!

I was asked to be a camp counselor for a girls' cabin, a journalist for the camp newspaper and a pianist for chapel services. Yes, I did play the piano, but needed music most of the time. And they asked me to be a rifle instructor--*yes, you read that correctly.* My brothers taught me how to shoot a rifle, target practice only of course. I thoroughly enjoyed each task … most weeks.

At that time in our culture, guys and girls "dated" as a way of doing things together—sporting events, water skiing, swimming, picnics, musical events, and youth activities. The list was endless. Guys and girls generally did not do things in groups, rather on a "date."

I lived nearly nineteen miles from Orlando, which was where more fun things were happening. It was great to have a guy friend drive me, share food, and take me home. I counted twenty-six different guys up to this point in my teen life that I had "dated."

It will seem strange in our current culture, but I had made a strong decision to do what I was taught a godly teen should do. *Remain sexually pure until God brings the man of his choice into your life, and you marry him.* My parents graciously supported this view. They helped me see the value in waiting.

I chose to follow that guideline because not only did I want to please God, but I grasped the value in it. So, if a "date" decided to drive to an isolated spot, turn off the car motor and move in my direction in the front seat, I firmly told him of my decision to save my body for my husband. If the conversation went deeper, I assured him, if and when he became my husband, it would then be time for us to go further.

Not here. Not now.

It was not always easy.

Years later when I learned my mother's story, I more clearly understood my parents's fervent desire for me to remain sexually pure for marriage. I am sure that led them to pray much for me. *I will be eternally grateful for their role in presenting this desirable lifestyle.*

———

So that summer at camp, I was determined not to be distracted in anyway by guys.

There were banquets at the end of each camp week. There

were drives into Gainesville for a break between camp sessions. There was free time with opportunities for getting acquainted with other staff. Keeping this in moderation provided adequate time with campers in the daily routine of camp. The summer had gone well for me, and I was feeling joy for the time I devoted to campers.

The last two weeks of 1966 summer camp were approaching with co-ed high school campers. I was a senior camp counselor for a girls' cabin. In addition, the building where I worked on the camp newspaper was down near the waterfront. It also provided waterfront items, such as lifejackets, boat cushions, canoe paddles, fishing poles for counselors who held sessions on the waterfront.

It seemed each day when I went down to the small office, one of the camp counselors for a boy's cabin who taught canoeing came in. After teaching canoeing and bringing the supplies back, Jim asked questions about the newspaper. Before long I suggested he write an article for the paper. No matter how gently or strongly my invitation was given, he declined.

I was mystified.

The second and last week of high school camp, conversations with this guy counselor seemed to increase. There was a good rhythm between us. I enjoyed those sessions. My first impression was, *he is so friendly.* Everyone thought so. It was a nice break in the day to hear his laughter as he talked about fun incidents with campers.

The final day of summer camp ended, as each week of summer camp did, with a banquet. Somehow, I ended up sitting across from him.

After campers went back to their cabins he asked, "Are you staying with staff to help close up the camp for the winter?"

"Yes, for both days."

"Would you like to go into Gainesville tomorrow with me? Maybe to have dinner?"

"Sure, Jim. That would be a nice break after all summer here."

Even in our tiredness, the conversation brought laughter and joy. It had been a great summer, a blessed two final weeks. After dinner he asked, "How are you planning to get back home? Could I drive you? Orlando is on the way to my home on the coast."

I agreed.

We seemed to never run out of things to talk about, laugh about and simply enjoy. It had been a full summer for me, and a full two-weeks for him. It was a wonderful way for us to "unwind" before we had to re-enter our respective schools and work back home. I was beginning to *feel something* when I was with Jim. Should I listen to those feelings? Or would he eventually think, *I don't want you.*

———

Once I was home again, I rested and thanked God for a great summer. I felt God kept me focused on serving the campers and blessing other counselors as best I could. Campers made decisions to begin learning more about Jesus, to follow Jesus, and some to serve Him.

My own faith was strengthened.

That experience confirmed my interest in following Jesus more intimately. That is, learning more about him and the relationship I – *a woman* – could have with him. It was great being with others who wanted it too.

I was beginning to believe Jesus truly did love me – *just as I am?*

Is it possible Jesus wants *me?*

Even if others *don't* want me?

That was the piece of music I wanted to keep playing.

Chapter 7

In His Own Words

A week later the phone rang. As I heard the coins dropping into a pay phone, I wondered who would be paying to talk with me.

"Where are you calling from?"

"Satellite Beach. It is Jim from summer camp."

I smiled. I loved hearing his voice. I enjoyed the chat.

Our conversation ended with a clear question, "Would you go out with me next weekend?" It was a two-hour drive from the coast. He could come early evening and return to his home the same night. He had my attention. He must like me if he is willing to drive all that way. I liked being with him. Feelings surfaced *again.*

Who is this Jim? Perhaps I should learn more.

That fall provided several opportunities.

—

This is Jim's recollection of meeting Bev—in his own words.

My first recollection of stepping on Camp Horizon soil was after seeing a girl walking across the field, saying to myself, "Self, you need to get to know that young lady." I remember the first week being frustrated because you kept hanging around another guy. As that first week ended, I discovered the other guy was your brother! Then I decided "to move in for real."

As the last week of summer approached, I wanted to ask you to the final banquet. When it was announced this was "Sadie Hawkins Day," I knew girls got to ask the guys. I kept trying to bump into you, so you would ask me.

In the meantime, a camper snagged me. But surprisingly, when we sat down at the banquet table, you were directly across from me. So, we were able to talk face to face instead of side by side. Then Bill sang 'First Love.'"

I drove you to your home in Orlando.

I wrote you letters.

I called on the pay phone—using my weekly tip money for carrying groceries to people's cars at Publix grocery store. I was able to drive to see you in Orlando about twice a month. We went to musical performances, football games, restaurants, and once even went bowling with your parents—what fun!

All these events we did in my hot car—an old SIMCA. I took it in for repair on a Thursday. The repair guy said it would be ready on the following Monday morning. That was January. I got it back in April. I drove it to college the next day and had to put in five quarts of oil on the way home. It only held three quarts. I returned it. In the meantime, the repair guy loaned me an old Ford station wagon that burned so much oil, he saved the oil from other cars to put in it. It had a hole in the top of the radiator that had been there so long that it rusted the top of the hood. Every now and then rusty water would spray out of there and cover the whole car. Steam out the front and smoke out the back.

I wondered how this would impress you.

… His own words.

Whew! There is more.

… My words.

Chapter 8

That Letter

Letters continued coming, the normal way to communicate long distance back then.

In December 1966, I received a letter from Jim that got my attention.

In *that* letter Jim told me he wrote to his parents in Canada, to say he had met "a girl just like the girl that married dear ole' dad." *That* sounded serious.

As the new year unfolded, my focus was on school, job, youth activities, and a fervent desire to grow in relationship with God.

I never wanted to "lead Jim on." I wanted to be truthful about my intentions. Yet, this was not the timing I imagined. I wanted to finish my dream of going to college first. Or was I dreaming? I began praying more intently. I felt I needed to change the caution light to either red or green. I needed more time. I so enjoyed time with Jim. Yet, it seemed a bit premature for me.

I eventually made a list of characteristics I wanted in a life-long mate. *I know—it sounds weird.* I of course never actually expected any one human would have all these. I simply wanted to know what was most important. *How do you decide on a life-long mate when you are only 20 years old?*

As I recalled the many guys I knew, I listed qualities that I liked in all twenty-something-of-them—not more than one or two in each guy. *Was I looking for a Prince Charming?*

*Dream on, Bev! A*re you expecting from a future husband the impossible qualities you feel others are expecting from you? *You are not enough.* How often I felt others saw me that way. Am I going to give him the very words that have stabbed me?

I decided to seriously look at this list of characteristics I admired and wanted in a life-long mate. As I thought about Jim and how I had gotten to know him, I began checking qualities I saw in him. Surprised? Oh my ... *All* these qualities in one human being! Could it be *that this human being was the one* with whom God had prepared me to spend the rest of my life?

Oh my... speechless ....

—

May 14, 1967. Jim and I enjoyed sitting alongside Lake Eola in Orlando. Jim asked my engagement and wedding ring choice from a catalog he brought.

We laugh today when we acknowledge there was not the drum roll, or the video production for the world to witness at the "asking of my hand in marriage."

Because it did not happen—not overtly, not officially. No, he did not actually propose.

However, once the rings arrived on June 3, the engagement ring was placed on my left finger. It was official and joy filled the atmosphere. We were both ecstatic. Who gets to spend the rest of her life with "the love of her life?" I could hardly sleep. How do you describe the joy, the love, the hope as you count down to *the day?* We set the wedding date for a time when his parents could come down from Canada to attend—after Christmas that year, December 29, 1967.

Jim and I now engaged, were both excited about spending the summer of 1967 at Camp Horizon in Orange Springs, Florida. I was Head Girls Counselor and Jim was Head Boys Counselor. Our tasks varied, as they did each summer. I especially enjoyed playing the piano for chapel services because Jim led the singing. It was fun and fulfilling.

That summer seemed to pass quickly and found us ready to move forward with fall plans, counting down to the wedding. We both found jobs. Jim traded in the SIMCA at the car rental for a Chevy Malibu 1966. He was given $150 for the SIMCA, although later when the car dealer saw the actual SIMCA, he said he did not know how he would get that much for it. It had served its purpose. Jim attracted a girl who clearly did not marry him for his sporty car!

I met Jim's Scottish parents two days before the wedding, after they came down from their home in Burlington, Ontario, Canada. I often said, "I am not marrying his family, so it is okay to meet them two days before the wedding. I am so glad they can come down." This gives you a bit of insight into my naiveite regarding family dynamics.

Our wedding was all that I had hoped for and more. When I was in junior high school and first learned my dad had heart problems and associated pain, I began praying he would live long enough to give me away at my wedding. God answered that prayer, and it was a highlight for me. The wedding was in the evening in Orlando at our church. Friends of many years attended it, along with Jim's church family in Bethany-by-the Sea from Satellite Beach. Our siblings were groomsmen and bridesmaids, plus my best friend, Lois. Jim's Uncle Dan Snaddon who pastored in Satellite Beach, led the service.

"May I introduce to you, Mr. and Mrs. Jim Hislop ...."

Our first home, January 1968, was back at Camp Horizon in Orange Springs, Florida, where we had first met. This multi-acre camp site on a beautiful lake, was virtually alone. Clear across the lake was a Girl Scout Camp that was used only a couple times a year when tents were brought in for a given week. There were no other facilities or landowners surrounding the lake. Our own Camp Horizon was empty throughout the off-season—and this was in the Florida climate. Jim and I wanted to open the facility for year-around retreats and other uses. This was welcomed by the board, and we moved into the small house near the front of the site.

Jim was accepted at the University of Florida (U of F) in Gainesville, yet when he registered for winter quarter courses, it was a surprise to learn that the courses were filled. So, we were able to spend the winter quarter (January – March) full-time at Camp Horizon.

This was our true "honeymoon." We had the lake and all

the boating options available to us. We could canoe, sail, ski, swim, play ball, or have our bare feet in the white lake sand.

A fun memory was when we had our first sailing experience in the camp's twelve-foot sailboat. It was *learning by experience* which we were both used to in life, so did not hesitate to give sailing a shot. We jumped on board and began our journey out into the big lake. As the wind grew stronger, we pulled harder on the main sheet. Slowly the boat seemed to be leaning increasingly sideways until it finally tipped completely over! It was so slow, if we had only known to do the opposite—release the main sheet that controls the boom on the main sail. Instead, we had a great twelve-foot mast on our capsized boat in a very shallow lake. Fortunately, Jim was a good swimmer, and he was able to swim onto shore and bring out the motorboat to pull us onto the shore. From then on, we let the sails tell us when to "come about" and when to let up on the main sheet.

It was a joy to host several retreats that spring. We served multiple roles each time and felt blessed to do so.

Early March 1968 Jim was able to get classes for spring term at the U of F.

Our living expenses were covered at the camp, however, there was no income per se. I was able to get a job as a Transcriptionist in the Purchasing Dept. at J. Hillis Miller Health Center at the U of F. I typed on a typewriter (no computers yet) orders for medicines—seven paper copies each order, with extensive and unfamiliar names of medicines. If a mistake was made, there were seven copies to correct—or start over with a fresh form.

When I told them I had to leave for summer camp, they said they would hold my job for the summer, if I would come back in the fall.

Surprised! *Really?* They *want* me?

During that summer camp season, Jim and I were Program Directors, while "Mr. and Mrs. G" where Camp Directors. This was a great fit and we thoroughly enjoyed serving with them. We felt immense joy at the end of the summer camp season.

We then drove to Canada to visit with Jim's parents for a good break before fall sessions.

As we headed back home, I anticipated going back to work and Jim attending U of F. It seemed a great fall was ahead of us.

After we sorted through the mail, we saw it, a letter from "Uncle Sam!"

> James Hislop Greetings, you are hereby ordered for induction into the Armed Forces of the United States, and to report at Cocoa Greyhound Bus Station, Cocoa, Florida on October 21, 1968, at 6 AM, for forwarding to an Armed Forces Induction Station.

We could not believe our eyes. Jim, a Canadian citizen, was drafted into the American Army? *Yes!* Don't anticipate joy or fun because you will be disappointed every time. *I should know better than to think more joy or fun awaited us.* Disappointed? *Yes!*

I thought surely God had slept through this one. *How could this be his will?* They held my job all summer for me. We had opened camp year-around for the first time. Would camp have to close again? *We were serving God!* I clearly did not understand this.

I went back to work at the J. Hillis Miller Health Center on the pre-determined date. I worked for two weeks and cried every day—before I could even tell them Jim was drafted. And I would have to leave. The job they held all summer for me, I would have to leave it.

I guess I would have to return to my parents' home in Orlando. My three siblings were still there. Where else would I go?

Was this all a dream? I was married, right? Nine months in paradise. And now I would have to go back to my family of six living together.

… Like a little girl again.

Our perfect world ended with "Uncle Sam's" letter.

... *That* letter.

Chapter 9

Goodbye and Hello

Goodbye was painful.

Months passed. I got a job. Life seemed to be in slow motion.

After basic training Jim was transferred to Redstone Arsenal in Huntsville, Alabama.

Jim took his sergeant's advice and signed up for Nike-Hercules Missiles training, which extended his time in Huntsville. Realizing our separation could be a year or more, Jim sought advice. His sergeant advised him to find a place for us to live and *then* tell his commander he was living off base.

He did.

We did. A small trailer in a trailer park. On the salary of a Private in the Army, what other options were there? It was truly a castle because we were together again.

I got temporary jobs with Manpower. We found a small church in the area and began making friends. Each day, each week, and each month were a joy, *being together again.*

—

One morning I woke up with stomach pain and vomiting. Was it flu? I had no other symptoms. It continued...and continued, every morning, for seven months.

Yes! We were expecting our first child. The joyful

anticipation was blurred each morning. We would have breakfast together. I was sure it would not happen *again this morning*. Jim would kiss me goodbye as he headed out to the base. I would run to the sink.

A new friend showed me how to fold a cloth diaper – no disposables back then. Buying baby bottles and pajamas had to be late afternoon events.

I was so eager to meet our precious new family member, while at the same time hoping my body would share that joy. The pain at one in the morning sent me to the U.S. Army Hospital at Redstone Arsenal. There was only one doctor on staff—but not on duty. A midwife was the one who tried to comfort me.

Loud screams throughout the morning, over and over. How could anyone sleep through that? She was forty-years old, waiting for her first child. She was next to me behind the curtain. My pain did not seem *that* bad. I thought they would send me home. Yet the midwife kept saying I should stay.

Family members—including husbands —were not allowed to enter the room. No cell phones—only the midwife could talk to the husband as he came into the building.

Finally. Seven p.m. *She came. Gorgeous. Precious.* Lots of mahogany brown hair already touching her shoulders. Blue eyes, yes, even a smile it seemed. Lorraine Marie Hislop. No baby on the planet could be this beautiful. And she was ours!

Each of the five days in that bed made me wonder if I would

ever get to go home. I only got to see and hold her when I was feeding her. *So lovable.* I did not want her to leave me – not ever! Why couldn't *I* bathe her and cuddle her? Why couldn't she sleep with me?

Not allowed in this hospital.

My husband was allowed to visit, but not when the baby was in the room. As he entered the first time, he rested his elbow on the bed, bent over to kiss the mother of his first child.

"Get out of here! Do not touch her!"

The midwife said *he was not to touch his wife?* I was ready to tell her how his wife got pregnant … but held my tongue.

He could see his daughter once each day by standing outside a glassed-in room with a sweeping video camera showing all the babies in the distance. He had no way of knowing which was his daughter.

Life back home was treasured. If Jim had not volunteered for the extra training—which meant longer military service time—he would not have been there at Lorraine's birth … Okay, maybe a few of our motorcycle rides together contributed to her coming early. Not sure…

Definitely an answer to prayer. What a gift, God. Thank you.

—

Only a week later we were on the road to Jim's parents' home in Canada. I had first met Willy and Mona the day before our wedding. They still had a strong Scottish brogue. I blushed and asked for a repeat, *repeatedly.*

Jim had to report to the Direct Support Platoon of 32nd ADDCOM in Karlsruhe, Germany right away. I could not accompany him. Not yet. I would live with Willy and Mona for now.

I was new at mothering. I felt very insecure. At least I had my own bedroom where I could feed her in private. Yet when I could not calm her down, I felt alone. Jim's younger brother David had an enthusiastic sense of humor and often brought a smile. Mitzie, their dog always tried to jump up to lick her face. Every meal was a treat and beautifully served. The best part was the ending with a Scottish cup of tea and crumpets, served in a fancy British cup and saucer. These dear in-laws were such a treasure during a challenging time.

Yet, Jim was in Germany. I was in Canada with a new baby, new in-law family, and their dog—new to me. Three months. Once again Jim was told to get housing, then report his living situation. He did.

Many Germans bought three floor apartments. Mom and dad on the first floor, married son or daughter on the second floor. They rented the third floor, at a reasonable rate for American military families. It had a living room, kitchen, two bedrooms, bathroom, and full closet. Laundry room was in the basement.

Now Jim was ready for us to join him.

By the time Willey and Mona drove me and baby Lorraine from their home in Burlington, Ontario to the JFK International Airport in New York, we were more than ready to be reunited in Germany.

Yet, there was still the nearly eight-hour flight to Frankfurt Airport. Our beautiful daughter was dressed in a striking new outfit, ruffles, lace – looked like a princess. She was ready to be reunited with her daddy. A moment to be celebrated!

Little did this naive new mother (me) know how many diapers would need to be changed, including overflow onto that "striking new outfit" during the eight-hour flight. That was like a full day. What a ride! The last packed diaper was now on. It was covered with the last packed jumpsuit. There was nothing else clean in the bag when her mom walked her off the plane into the arms of her excited daddy.

Not exactly dressed for a royal arrival. Yet, it felt like a royal arrival. Squeals. Hugs. Kisses. Smiles. Laughs. Everything but the music…

Never mind the baby's stains.

The nearly two-hour drive to our new home in Karlsruhe seemed like a blink.

Safe. *We were together again.*

A blessed "hello!"

Chapter 10

Heavy Boots on the Steps

I heard heavy boots on the steps.

I stopped.

A knock on our third-floor apartment door.

"Are you Spec 4 Hislop's wife? There has been an accident. We do not know any details, but we can come back in one hour to drive you to the U. S. Army Hospital in Heidelberg."

As the two officers left, I fell into a heap.

What happened? Was Jim dead? I was numb. No details?

The hospital was nearly an hour away. Two hours before I would know.

"Oh God. *Help!*"

I would ride with the two officers in their car, wondering if I would come back alone. Germany was beautiful, but when you did not speak the language, what help was there? *What if ...?* No cell phones or internet in the seventies.

"Oh God. Help."

We lived "on the economy." We rented that lovely third floor of a German home. I was grateful to be with my husband. Viet Nam was the nucleus of military draftees. We were so grateful he was not sent there. He was trained on the Nike-Hercules

Missiles. They were in Europe, so was he. It seemed a "safe" place. How could he have been injured?

Not here. Not now!

A dear friend came and kept baby Lorraine. I did not know when I would be back home. Again, it would be at least *two hours* before I would know *anything.*

———

While waiting, my thoughts began to revisit some of the experiences we had while living there. Soon after our arrival in Germany, we went on Sundays to hear Chaplains talk about stars and galaxies. Yes, stars and galaxies. We were hoping for words about God spoken in English.

We eventually found the only option, Karlsruhe Baptist Church. We were not Baptists, but they spoke English. The pastor left the church before we got there. He was not paid enough, so he spent the next six months traveling around Europe before returning to the U.S.

We loved this new experience. There were people from nearly twelve denominations represented. It forced us to make the main thing the main thing. What do you believe about God? About Jesus? About the Holy Spirit? Each week someone different from the elder team led the service.

Friends were easy to make. They all spoke English.

"Where y'all from?" had to be the South. It was. Georgia, Alabama, South Carolina …. Florida was not really considered "the south," since many moved from the northern United States to Florida. After lots of practice even I could say it, "Where y'all from?"

The Sunday service was all they had. I so wanted to sit down with some other women and hear more about their faith experiences. I wanted to learn more about the Bible.

Once when I was reading the Bible at home alone, I thought it said women could teach. Immediately a voice in my head said, *Bev, do you think you know more than the leaders in your church?* Of course not, end of conversation.

On a trip to Heidelberg one day, we stopped at a bookstore that carried books written in English. I found a commentary on a book in the New Testament. I purchased it. Every day I read one chapter. My appetite grew. I wanted more. I wanted to hear input from others on what this book said. All I knew to do was to ask God. Several weeks went by. I finished the book. Now what?

The next Sunday a woman came up to me. "Bev, have you ever thought of having some women get together and have a Bible study?" I was speechless for a few seconds.

"Yes! Yes! Yes, Cindy!"

"Well, umm, let's do it then."

"You can come to my house. I will make refreshments. I will get a babysitter." I blurted out.

Two weeks later my small living room began to fill with

women. After we all introduced ourselves, Cindy looked at me and said, "Okay Bev, it's time to start."

"Start? What do you mean?"

"Bev, you can begin leading us now."

"What? I don't know how to lead!" *I am not enough.* "I thought you would lead."

"Me? I cannot lead! Anyone here want to lead?"

Dead silence.

"Well, what do you want to study? Anything particular in the Bible?"

Silence.

"Well, how about a book in the New Testament? I Corinthians?" That was the book I had been reading for several months.

"Sure. Will you lead us then, Bev?"

I was shaking. One part of me was so excited to see the possibility of my dream come true. Yet another part could not imagine leading. I had never done this before. *I am not enough, remember....* Yet my heart so wanted it that I felt in the moment I must take the risk.

"Okay then, I will on one condition. We will each read a chapter in I Corinthians during the week and then when we get together, we all will bring questions and contribute to the conversation. I cannot do this alone. But I would love to hear from each of you. I would love to hear more of your faith in God."

The enthusiasm expressed by each woman, along with the prevailing desire for such an experience carried me along. Preparing refreshments, getting the babysitter and our daughter ready, cleaning the house, setting up the living room chairs ... whew! Soon I learned that doing it all *plus* leading the study was not the best plan. *Save that wisdom for later.*

I did not serve Kool-Aid, but *the babysitter* did wipe little noses.

Was it truly acceptable for me to love learning about Jesus from the Bible by studying and teaching others?

My heart opened. My faith deepened. My soul soared.

And I began to experience the truth. "I press on to take hold of that for which Christ Jesus *took hold of me.*" (Philippians 3:12) I took you, Bev.

Christ Jesus through his Holy Spirit is enough.

—

Still waiting ... Back to reality.

Would Jesus through his Holy Spirit be enough again? Now?

Two of the longest hours *ever.* For sure.

*Finally...*heavy boots on the steps. *Again.*

A knock on the door. *Again.*

I thought this hour would never come.

I opened the door, purse in hand.

"I'm ready."

"Okay, let's go down to the car."

"Have you heard anything about how my husband is doing?"

"No."

It was a long hour's drive. I sat in the back seat. The sergeants in the front seat talked.

As we walked down the hospital corridor, the sergeants approached the emergency counter. They were talking to the nurse.

All I could hear was a woman in agonizing pain, screaming non-stop, sobbing. Would she catch a breath? Was she dying? Were they cutting her open?

"What happened?" I asked a sergeant.

"The doctor worked on her husband before he finished with your husband. Her husband did not make it. They said it would be a few more minutes before we could see Jim."

Oh Lord! Someone else was more important than my husband? Why would a doctor have to choose between two husbands, two soldiers?

"Oh God. *Help!*" God gave me my precious husband. Would God take him away... to heaven? Now? My husband? *Oh God!* Help.

The hospital nurse startled me by saying, "You can go see your husband now."

He must be breathing. He must be alive.

I could hardly breathe as I walked down the corridor.

There he is. Sitting up in a chair. He has his clothes on. His face looks alive. His body is attached. *What happened?* Then he held out his hand. It was wrapped in white.

"You are sitting up?" The expression on my face surprised him. "I thought …" The death screams in the hallway were still heavy. "I thought …"

"The doctor was ready to sew the tip of my finger back on but had to leave to attend to three life-threatening emergencies. By the time he came back to me, he said it was too late to re-attach my finger. He severed the tip of it. I am simply waiting for them to release me."

"I did not know. Your sergeant said he did not know. How did it happen?"

"When I drove Ken's Volkswagen Bug to pick up our mail, the choke got hung up a few times. As I cleared it, my gloved hand got caught between the fan belt and the generator pulley wheel. I extracted it, but with great pain. I put the blood-filled glove back on. I was able to quickly drive back to the Unit. The sergeant jumped over the desk when he saw it and took me at once to the dispensary. Only to have the doctor say I needed to go to the Heidelberg Hospital. An ambulance transported me—with a medic aboard in case I went into shock."

Obviously, this surprise far exceeded my expectations.

I was so grateful for Jesus hearing me and taking care of Jim.

I was so excited to have him back home with us.

Jesus met me in my expectations. Jesus is enough.

Soon Jim began the journey of retraining that shortened finger to jump up to hit the o and p on the typewriter.

Fortunately, those heavy boots were not on our steps *again*.

Chapter 11

Over and Out

Jim never came home from the military base in the middle of the day.

Something major must be wrong.

After running up the stairs to our third-floor apartment, Jim was out of breath. He entered looking a bit pale. He asked me to sit down. His words were hard for me to process. He repeated them... *again.*

"The Red Cross called the Karlsruhe Military Base and said Ray--your dad--died. We can arrange a call on Base with your mom."

—

"Mom, what happened? –over-and-out."

"Heart surgery was a success, but his lungs collapsed. Your Dad's memorial service is next week. Don't worry about coming. The family is here, and everything is taken care of … oh, over-and-out."

"But Mom, I want to come. I will try to get a flight –over-and-out."

That is all I remember of that over-and-out call.

—

I checked every airline that flew from Frankfort, Germany to the U.S. The earliest flight I could get would not leave for a few weeks. Seems unbelievable in today's world. Jim only had three months of military service left. He could not leave. I would have to go by myself.

We lived off base. No cell phones, no internet. There was a three-year waiting list for a land-line phone. Letters took one to two weeks to arrive. I wondered every day and night how Mom was doing. Her greatest fear had become a reality. Her husband was no longer with her.

I remembered when Dad had one of the early artificial heart valves implanted, six years previously. For three months after the implant, Dad said every time he took a breath, the incision from throat to belly button hurt. He never wanted his chest cut open again. He was not awake to decide this time.

I finally got a flight home to Florida. I wondered how I could fly alone with our active twenty-one-month-old daughter, while nauseated with a second pregnancy.

The flight from Frankfort to New York was filled with military spouses and kids. I wrapped little surprises—toys, sweets, books—for Lorraine to open along the way. Once she "got it" she was too excited to wait for the next one. Within a couple of hours, they were all opened and set aside. The military doctor gave me a couple of pills to help her to sleep on this flight. They made her hyperactive.

The short flight from New York to Florida seemed

even longer. Would she ever sleep? *Finally.* Just as the pilot announced we were landing at MCO, Orlando .... *Oh yeah,* asleep just as we landed.

But so worth it. I loved being with family again. *Had it really been two years?* The last time was cemented in my mind from a picture of me pregnant in front of our house trailer in Huntsville, Alabama, standing beside Dad, Mom, and sister Carole. They stopped by on their way home from visiting family in Indiana.

Our daughter Lorraine was their only grandchild. She was born with a sweet smile, and loving eyes. Dad had seen pictures of her—which Mom told me he showed to everyone he could. He was counting the days to seeing her in person, to holding her.

Now that would never happen.

I was glad to hear Dad's father, Clarence White plus Aunt Gwen and Uncle Ollie Allen were able to come from Indiana for Dad's funeral in Orlando. Gwen was Grampa's last living child. She would be the only one to outlive Grampa—not even her husband did.

"Grampa took it pretty hard ..." Mom's letter said. What parent wants to see his child die—no matter the age? My dad was only 49 years old.

———

By the time I arrived, most of the family's community life had moved on. The funeral happened a couple of weeks before. There was no hint that Mom's love-of-her-life was no longer present. No one talked about it. *None of us understood the grief process.* Friends and family simply tried to "move on." It seemed that was what you did.

Soon after, my three siblings married the one each was close to. Mom attended each wedding alone. She wondered if Ray was watching from above.

God help me. I could not "move on." The reality was just beginning to hit me. Because I was not at his funeral, I did not see his body, his casket or hear the service. Were the people who attended the service trying to be happy because he was in heaven? Or did they tear up when they saw the reality right in front of them? I saw no indicators.

I had none of those advantages. At first, I thought that was a good thing. I missed the hard part—seeing the casket, feeling the pain of loss and tears. The reality had not yet arrived.

In fact, that first night my dad walked into my bedroom.

"I thought you were dead!"

"No, I'm here!"

I was so excited. I got up to walk out with him, only to wake up and realize *once again* it was just a dream. He really was *not* going to physically walk out of that room with me.

He was *not* going to encourage me to play the piano, while he sang.

He was *not* going to ask my opinion on his writings.

He was *not* going to share his life stories.

Not laugh together. *Not* cry together. *Not* pray together.

For two years I dreamed the same dream.

—

The impact of the hole was slowly seeping in. I had not been there to see his dead body. My siblings and life-long friends saw him.

It was later that I learned the artificial heart valve that was inserted six years prior was only guaranteed to last five years, six at the most. We were in year six.

My dad was a great teacher at church and had a caring heart for people. There was a Saturday church youth group boating/skiing event at Lake Cain near Orlando. One of the youths jumped into the water from the boat. No one could see Dennis in the water. But blood was surfacing. His body and boat rudder collided. Immediate intervention was too late. Dennis died.

This reality soon led my dad and my mom to Dennis' parents's home. *How tragic. How do you comfort parents in this pain?* Soon, another church leader came by. It was not long before Dad whispered to Mom, "We need to leave now."

Dad asked Mom to drive. Once in the car, he said, "My heart valve has stopped. I love you." They raced home. The 911 call brought an ambulance, which took him to the hospital. Such heart surgeries were relatively new in Orlando at the time.

Mom sat in the waiting room. A couple of Dad's colleagues came by and waited. Then left. Mom waited all night. Alone.

At 5:30 a. m. the surgeon walked in to say, "The surgery was a success." Sigh. "However, the patient's lungs collapsed. He didn't make it."

Can you imagine? Being there alone, *hearing that the love of your life has just died!*

Mom drove home all alone. Inside the house my siblings were in bed. Mom simply knocked on each door and said, "He didn't make it."

Silence.

Mom collapsed on her bed. *Alone.*

None of us understood grief.

—

Years later I would understand that we were all still in Stage One of the grief process: Protest. Disoriented. Numb. "Nothing is wrong. I am fine." Accepting the reality of the loss was only the beginning. Understanding and processing all five stages took time. They eventually did bring healing. 1

I did not realize at the time how blessed I was to arrive at Mom's home six weeks after Dad's death. It was a gift to both of us to begin talking about this unbelievable tragedy.

Did it really happen? Would we never see him again on this earth?

Just then, twenty-one-month-old Lorraine would come running in the room with a giggle. She brought instant joy, for a few minutes. Then as she went back to her doll, I looked at the tears running down Mom's cheeks.

"Ray would have loved to see her, to play with her. Why was he not given that joy?"

"I do not know. I wish we could bring him back, don't you?" I replied.

"I know we will see him in heaven, but that could be a long time. I am only forty-seven."

I was almost twenty-five.

Would we ever be able to fill that empty place in our lives?

—

I remembered as a little girl my mom read a children's pictorial version of Bible stories each evening. The night I saw the picture of Jesus' arms stretched out and feet hanging down, both nailed to a wooden cross, I asked, "Why is he hanging there? Doesn't that hurt?"

She said, "It was for you."

"For me? What do you mean, Mom?"

"We were all born needing forgiveness for the things we do wrong, for our sins. Jesus, who never sinned, came down to this earth for the purpose of telling us, 'God loves you and Jesus paid the price for your forgiveness.' He gave his life for us. All we must do is accept Jesus into our lives."

"How Mom? I want to."

"Jesus loves you, Bev. Simply ask Jesus to forgive you for all your sins. Tell Him you love him. And thank Him for giving His life for you. Ask Him to come into your heart."

I did.

The peace and joy in my five-year-old heart was impactful and memorable.

—

Then memories of my fifteenth birthday surfaced. I was given permission to wear "high heels" by my dad and mom. That made me an adult woman, I surmised. It seemed like a big deal.

That was when our family moved on from a house church to a bigger church. And being baptized was an important public event. I still believed that at least Jesus loved me. I was told I needed to publicly say those words. I did.

The poem my dad wrote for me that day hangs on my bedroom wall today. It was one of the great gifts he gave me.

To Bev, on Her Fifteenth Birthday

Today our daughter's walking tall
With new hose, high heels, and all!
This is the day, so hold your spleen,
Bev White is now a grand fifteen!

With grownup airs and fancy ways,
You sweetly pass the waiting days
To adulthood – you're three-fourths between,
For today you've reached a full fifteen!

We wish the very best for you,
May it always be said that Bev is true,
Kind-hearted and fine, but never mean,
The things expected from a girl fifteen!

For the future, then, as you look ahead,
'Woman of wisdom,' may it ever be said.
Spirit-filled and led, may you always be seen,
As sweet as when you were just fifteen!

From your dad (Raymond V. White 12.10.61)

God how can life go on without my dad?

… Over and out.

Being God's Dearly Loved

Being God's dearly loved means letting the truth of our *being dearly loved* become enfleshed in everything we think, say, or do. It typically comes in four phases.

1. Taken 2. Chosen. 3. Broken. 4. Given

—

2. CHOSEN

"I have chosen you and have not rejected you." (Isaiah 41:9)

Really?

God chose *me*?

How can I close the gap between who I believe I am and who God says I am?

The gap is wide.

I believe what people say or think about me.

I want to begin listening more consistently to who God says I am.

That is who I want to be.

But *that* seems impossible for me.

Chapter 12

Thanksgiving Baby

"Get ready, you will have a Thanksgiving baby." The doctor gave us good news.

Not December. There were multiple events in December— in addition to Christmas and New Year's Eve. My birthday, my sister's birthday, our wedding anniversary plus friends' birthdays.

That sounded like good news. Until Thanksgiving came … and went. Danny was not ready to join us on the earth. Not yet. My calculations said he was advancing toward a ten-month in utero life. *Oh my…* Fortunately, the nausea and vomiting had stopped a couple of months before. Now it was simply discomfort.

We were so excited to have a son. Our dream was to have one daughter and one son. *Who gets their dream?*

We did. December 23, 1971. I was only in the hospital a couple of days. Jim could be there right after the birth. It was so good to be in the USA again. Jim's military service was completed. We were back in Florida. The nurses put Danny in a Christmas stocking and sent us home Christmas Day. What a gift, best son ever! His older sister loved having a baby to cuddle and show him the world. She had two years and three months experience and expertise.

They were truly Thanksgiving babies. *We were giving thanks.*

Two preschoolers in our small mobile home, at Lucky Clover Trailer Park in Melbourne Florida. Naps were not their favorite part of the day. Rather, lots of activity: laughing, running, cycling, swinging, and swimming in our small above ground pool outside.

Suddenly I heard cries and screams. *Fear gripped my heart.* I ran outside to see blood in the water. She decided to jump backwards from a small chair she set outside the pool. A jump into the twelve-inch-deep pool had somehow cut her bottom lip. I collected our daughter. Took her to the doctor.

She was so brave. I managed to get her there without fainting. I waited behind the doctor while he stitched her up. I was reminded of how faint I felt seeing my dad in a hospital bed. So, I didn't look at the blood. I was relieved when the doctor was done. *I made it.* I was able to drive her home.

It wasn't long before we returned to have the stitches removed. I again took my side position. I figured if I made it through the initially painful procedure, certainly removing the stitches would be easy.

The stitches were all out. She made it. *I made it.*

As the nurse was getting Lorraine ready to sit up and leave, the doctor walked over to me, put the bloody stitches into my hand.

What? A souvenir? Really?

You guessed it.

I fainted.

You are not enough as a mom. Your daughter was hurt, and *you fainted?*

—

Danny was the first one out the door most days. Lorraine not so much. She needed to get ready for kindergarten. We were the security trailer for Sea Park Elementary School in Satellite Beach, Florida. The huge empty ditch outside our home was an exciting playground for Danny. Hiding, throwing the ball, fighting, building forts, sailing boats … quite a list of creative ventures each day. Some days with a friend. Some days with water in the ditch.

The biggest challenge came at changing the morning schedule to get him ready for kindergarten. Older sister was already into the routine, starting second grade. After school, Danny was ready to start riding his bicycle around the pavement. The cars would have to wait for him. Speed was his gig.

Danny raced his bike up and down the stretch of ground. *Oops.* A rock in the way? His bike fell with him on it. He was bleeding. By the time Jim ran over to him, Danny was still waiting. He couldn't find his mom who saw him first.

She had fainted.

You are not enough as a mom. Your son was hurt, and *you fainted.*

Danny was not even crying.

A few stitches and the guys went home smiling.

—

How does a new mother navigate life with two precious, loveable preschoolers? I guess I missed the training. Surely someone who has older children could give me help.

I asked a woman I admired at church. She had four children. She said we should go to the only women's weekly gathering. Perhaps someone there could give us input.

We went. We listened. Eventually the leader asked, "Are there any more prayer requests?" My friend then raised her hand and asked, "Could we pray for us new mothers?"

The leader responded. "You can pray for your kids at home. We are here to pray for the missionaries."

We were stunned! *We don't want you* surfaced yet again.

Because I shared my need with this dear mother of teens, we both agreed to pray for each other. What would other women do with personal prayer needs? This brief scenario sent a lasting desire to provide more for women in the church context.

Little did I know the journey ahead.

Chapter 13

No Milk for the Kids

No milk for the kids?

Our monthly income was simply "the offering" taken the first Sunday of the month. At times we were short, other times a bit over. We navigated as best we could to maintain a balanced budget. Summer was especially challenging because people were on vacation. But it was not summer.

We were out of milk.

This was a first for us. We had moved to the Orlando area for Jim's new job as the church "full-time worker" (other churches would call him a pastor). This was his sole employment, our sole income. Most months we managed well.

I began praying. "Lord, would you please give us money for milk? Our kids need a good breakfast before going to school tomorrow."

I did not know what else to do.

Months before, I verbalized my dream of taking credit courses at the local community college. With both kids in school and Valentia Community College (VCC) close by, it seemed a suitable time. After Jim agreed, I began praying more intensely for funds. We both acknowledged the money would need to come beyond our monthly income. That would be confirmation of God's will for me at this point in life. *Should I* in faith *register?* I did.

And now we do not have enough money for a gallon of milk for our kids.

What was I thinking? The desire for more schooling surfaced even more intensely. *Don't anticipate this as joy or fun because you will be disappointed every time.*

That evening at church a woman came up to me and said, "Bev, here is what I owe you. I'm so sorry it's so late." She put five dollars in my hand. "What do you owe me for?" She looked surprised and said, "Um, I don't remember. I just *know* that I owe you five dollars."

Milk was on the table for breakfast the next morning.

Oh, Lord, you heard my prayer. Was she an angel? I do not know. *Did you, Lord, tell her to give me five dollars?*

—

The next morning as I was reading Acts, I found myself wondering, "Does God's Spirit speak to us today?" How else would we know to do God's will? Is that how she knew to give me five dollars at *that* time?

Jesus told us once he ascended into heaven he would send his Holy Spirit to us—which he clearly did, and we read about it in Acts. *It was so exciting.* As I began to enter more fully into that possibility and what it might mean for me today, a thought suddenly shut that door. *Bev, do you think you know more than your church elders who clearly believe God's Spirit does not speak to us today?*

Of course not. End of conversation.

—

My desire to continue in college would not go away.

Was this God's will? How could I know for sure?

Funds continued to be lacking.

Until the final date of registration for one course. The exact amount arrived *that day.*

The excitement of the first day of class was also filled with nervousness. I was so much older than most students and it had been a few years since I had been in school. *Could I do it? Would I fit in?* Or would I hear again, *we don't want you!*

The first morning of the class, I sat down in the hallway waiting for the class door to open. Within a few minutes, I noticed someone sitting next to me with the same textbook opened. I turned and asked if she was taking the class. She said, "Yes. But it has been a long time since I've been in school, so I'm nervous."

"Really? How long?"

"Well, my kids are in junior high school."

"Where?"

"Robinswood Junior High School."

"So are mine!"

Before long, we discovered we were both followers of Jesus going back to school after years at home. *God you are amazing.* Tuition plus a great friend.

God opened all the needed doors—in his perfect timing. At least for that first VCC course. Would the funds come in *again?* A new challenge each semester.

> I wrote in my journal: "I will extol the Lord at all times; his praise will always be on my lips." (Psalm 34:1)

———

A couple of days later Jim walked in with a check for $150 from a friend. I was speechless. Neither of us expected it. Yet God knew. "Lord, you have answered, and I thank you for stretching my faith, but also for being faithful and answering that prayer, again."

June 1983. I received my Associate in Arts degree from Valentia Community College.

Would you believe it? *Believe it. God did it.*

Am I becoming who God says I am? Taken. Chosen. *Chosen!*

> "You did not choose me, but I chose you and appointed you so that you might go and bear fruit—fruit that will last—and so that whatever you ask in my name the Father will give you." (John 15:16)

What an amazing God…he chose me!

—

"God, you continue stretching my faith. You want me to trust you, no matter what."

Could I trust God to provide much-needed recreation time with our two teenagers? And Jim needing to relax and have fun too? We loved the water, especially skiing and boating.

"But, Oh Lord, I could not imagine owning a boat! That would not even be spiritual, *right?* Yes, I would love that for our family, but it costs. There is only one way that would ever happen—y*ou, God!*"

We began praying in March. We prayed that all the money that came in that month from outside sources would indicate God's leading.

The Lord sent the unheard amount of $1200! *Really?* How much clearer could this be? The Lord led us in the maze of finding a dependable boat plus funds for all the equipment needed – all within a month. "What a joy to see you, Lord, provide sunny Florida weather and relaxation for our family all at the same time." *Joy indeed.*

Imagine. God provided the money that one month we prayed—for a specific desire. "Lord, you are an amazing God who does care. You care even about our need to relax, and refresh as a family. Thank you, Lord!"

That amount above our monthly income was not seen again.

God was teaching me lessons I would need throughout the rest of my life.

God is bigger than our needs—and even our desires.

Bigger than a gallon of milk. Bigger than a boat? Whew...

When the desire is from God, he will provide, in his time and his way.

.... I wish I had more fully embraced those lessons in the days ahead.

Chapter 14

I Am Not Enough

"Women aren't home during the day," they responded.

"Who would we invite in this neighborhood? I don't know anyone."

God, I thought you were laying this on my heart.

So, I continued praying. "Lord, I simply want your will in this, your timing, your choice participants." Some days it seemed more likely than others. Yet I continued praying and dropping seeds of thought as appropriate among the women.

I envisioned a "Ladies Coffee" at our current church in central Florida. Back then that term was in vogue and was a wonderful way to draw neighborhood women together. It included a relaxed "craft" that was demonstrated and reproduced. A short testimony and brief teaching followed. A program for young children was also included.

I continued praying. "Lord, this idea seemed new to these women. But since this is so heavy on my heart, I believe it is of you. I don't know how we would do this, but you do. Please bring together your choice women, with specific skills to implement this dream. Only you can make it a reality. In your time and your way."

Weeks went by. Months came and went. *Your time Lord?*

I was driving home. I heard a new voice on the Focus on the

Family radio program. It was an interview with Elisa Morgan, the first president of a growing organization, MOPS—Mothers of Preschoolers.

After I arrived home, the phone rang.

"Bev, I would love to do a children's program like MOPS when you start the Ladies Coffee." She was so excited. This dear woman was a recently retired kindergarten teacher. She heard the radio interview. She was more than qualified. And she loved children.

I was so excited that I began new conversations with a couple of women I saw as potential leaders for segments of the program. Each one said, "Yes."

Oh, Lord, is this your perfect timing?

The date was set. An incredible number of women came.

I was scheduled to speak after a testimony was given. I was left with only five minutes to share, "Walking with God."

I wrestled afterwards with the poor job I did. *I am not enough.*

"Forgive me, Lord. I trust you for the impact and results of that message. You have not allowed me to know and see them yet. But I want to just quietly hope and trust you for them. You have only asked me to be a clean, empty usable container. Fill me, Lord."

I began learning the key question was not, "Did I pull it off perfectly?"

Rather, "What did God's Spirit say?"

—

Women continued coming to develop friendships and learn about Jesus's love for them. Others developed leadership skills and growth in their faith.

I eventually learned that when God gives a vision, I simply begin praying and dropping seeds of thought. Even after I "cast the vision," there is likely the "death of a vision." It will seem it is not going to happen. That would leave me discouraged. The seeds were not taking root. And I would begin questioning my own vision, my motivation, and of course my abilities. *Don't anticipate this as joy or fun because you will be disappointed every time,* and *I am not enough* would surface *again.*

Eventually I realized that was part of the essential journey of the birth of a vision. God continually brought me to the place where I knew if it happened, it was God, not me. I did what God prompted me to do and trusted him to do what only he could do. I did not say it was easy waiting. God's timing was key. God worked behind the scenes in ways I was not even aware. When that day came, the pieces seemed to fall into place—not perfectly, but functionally.

—

It took more than one experience to teach me that. No experience had yet raised the level of angst that this new, surprising request did. Monday morning a phone call came from an unknown voice.

"Bev, I'm calling to ask if you would speak at our conference here in Hollywood, Florida." She asked if I would be *the main speaker.* My initial thought was to say, "No thanks, I have never done that. I am sure I couldn't." .... or something like that.

But before I could get those words out, a biblical text I had just read the night before sounded in my ear. It was from Exodus chapter four—Moses telling God what I wanted to tell the woman caller:

> "I have never been eloquent, neither in the past
> nor since you have spoken to your servant. I
> am slow of speech and tongue.... Please send
> someone else. (v. 10,13)

Only one thing stopped me. I never wanted to get to the point where God was angry with me.

"The LORD's anger burned against Moses..." (v. 14)

Would I believe God would do for me what he did for Moses?

"Now go; I will help you speak and will teach you what to say." (v. 12)

She was asking me to be *the only* speaker at a women's conference in south Florida. I had never, ever even thought of going beyond my local church and those responsibilities were challenging enough. So, I told her I would pray about it and get back with her. She asked me to do so within the week.

As soon as I hung up and told Jim, his immediate response was, "Well, you told her 'Yes,' didn't you?"

"*What?* Of course not. I should call her back and say I can't."

Jim was so affirming. I paused yet wrestled with the reality.

A few days later I called her back. Okay.... "I will."

———

I was sitting in the airport awaiting my flight to Hollywood. I looked up at the sign over the door: Hollywood, FL---an arrow to the right. Virginia Beach, VA—an arrow to the left. *I so wanted* to get up and go to Virginia Beach, where my mom was living.

Yet, I did not want to replay Jonah's story – I could not imagine a bed inside a whale. So, I waited and flew in just before the conference started. I had my briefcase, my high heels, and my suit on. *I looked official, right?*

I had every word written on paper and used them extensively —I so wanted to be sure every word was perfect. I was halfway through my first talk when my hand unconsciously moved onto the shelf inside the podium. I had no idea someone had kindly placed a glass of water there for me. Inadvertently, my hand knocked it over. Yes, it went down the front of my perfect outfitted suit.

I stopped. I did not know what to do.

I eventually regathered my thoughts and finished quickly.

I am not enough. *What a mess I am. See, God? I told you I*

could not do this. I want to fly home now. How will I sit through lunch and then give a second talk? I am done.

As I sat at the lunch table in the seat assigned me, I listened to the casual conversations all around me. I noticed the woman beside me was silent. I finally turned to her and asked her name. She told me. Then she said, "I want to thank you for spilling the water."

"What?" In my mind, *that* was the worst thing I did, and it showed what a failure I was. *How could she thank me?* Her words left me speechless.

"Bev, you seemed too perfect for me. I could not relate to you until you spilled the water. Then I knew you were human and maybe had something to say to me."

Oh God. I guess perfection is not what is needed. Show me what is.

—

A year later, I was asked to give a devotional at one of the few women's missionary conferences in Florida. I would speak for only fifteen minutes at 7:15 a.m. before the actual conference sessions began.

I knew God wanted me to accept, so I did.

Yet, anxiety visited all five months prior. What do I have to say to this group of older, mature women? I was much younger. I was not "a speaker" – certainly not like the ones they would hear at the rest of the conference. These were seasoned women on mission. *I am not enough.* I thought of calling and backing out. "I can't do this." There was plenty of time to find someone else.

Then God brought this verse back to my mind.

> "You did not choose me, but I chose you and appointed you so that you might go and bear fruit—fruit that will last—so that whatever you ask in my name the Father will give you." (John 15:16)

I knew this was God's plan for me. So daily I cried out to God. I felt so many negative emotions when I pictured myself up front. Yet, I sat with the Lord, waiting to hear what he wanted me to say for those fifteen minutes.

I arrived at the conference the night before, as did all the participants. I slept in a lodge onsite with other women. I only slept a couple of hours. I finally got up at 4:30 and went into the bathroom to throw up.

Yes! Vomit.

How will I do this? Oh Lord, how could this be your will? Once I get up front, I am sure I will forget everything ... Help me!

As I looked out at the crowd of women, God's all-consuming love for these women bombarded me. It was a new experience. *I felt a deep love for women I did not even know.* Everything in me wanted to express God's love for them in a way they would immediately embrace. Nothing else mattered at that moment.

My words: "Do you know how much God the father, Jesus Christ and his Holy Spirit *love you?* You are dearly loved! He loves you like no one in your life ever has or ever will. Jesus says this to you, 'God so loved the world that He gave his one and only Son, that whoever believes in Him, shall not perish but have eternal life.' (John 3:16) Do you believe Him? Jesus gave his life—literally—to redeem your choices in life..."

It was all about God. It was about these precious women who *Jesus loves.*

—

Once I finished speaking and sat down, I said to God, "Lord, if you ever ask me to do this again, I will say *yes* immediately! I have never felt you speak through me like that. I have never felt your Holy Spirit so engulf my mind, my heart, my spirit --- yes, even my body—at that precise moment. *Your* words, spoken through me. Hard to describe, a new experience, all fifteen minutes. It was a totally new experience.

I believe I am God's dearly loved daughter. *Chosen.*

Instead of the lie the enemy kept repeating in my head, *I am not enough,* the truth finally overtook the lie. *Jesus through his Holy Spirit* is *enough.*

> As I was with Moses, so I will be with you. I will never leave you nor forsake you. (Joshua 1:5b)

And God was certainly with me. And I knew—whatever the price—I wanted to experience more of his presence. I realized it was *not* about me being "enough."

Jesus through his Holy Spirit is enough!

.... If only I would have fully embraced that truth in the months ahead.

Chapter 15

I'm Too Excited

"I'm too excited."

"It can't be God's will for me."

"I want it too much."

Yes, I was excited about going to community college. And God sent the exact tuition amount just the day I needed it. *Every semester.* I knew it was God. I knew he wanted this for me. Yes, I had received my AA from VCC. *A dream came true.*

But that was only a pre-requisite to wanting to attend the University of Central Florida. I attended a semester in the fall of 1983 and the spring of 1984. What an enriching experience! I loved it. I so looked forward to taking more courses the next term.

Then it happened.

I registered for the next term. *I was excited.*

But after one week of classes, I withdrew.

The final payment was due, and the money was not there. Is this the death of a vision? I was excited about going. I loved school. It seemed perfect. Is this simply, *don't anticipate this as joy or fun because you will be disappointed every time? I am not enough.*

I grieved deeply. Extensively. *Where are you God?*

*Am I too excited about this Lord? Is that why you did not
send the money in time?*

—

Later that spring Jim and I attended a conference in Chicago.

On the way to the SCOPE conference, we passed through
Kokomo, Indiana. We were on the way to Knox to explore the
place of my "roots." We decided to get a motel for the night and
have a salad at Rax Restaurant.

Something was coming over Jim. He was beginning to like
this little farm town. Later he said, "If someone had come up
to me in the Rax Restaurant and ask if I would stay in Kokomo
and pastor their church, I would have said 'Yes! Send for our
kids.'"

We drove around and explored the city. Something was
going on inside of both of us, but we did not know what – *yet.*

The first speaker at the conference, Joe Aldrich, was
dynamite. The only problem? What he was saying was
too exciting. There really are opportunities for people who
want to mature spiritually and connect with others who do?
Opportunities for people who care about other people knowing
Jesus? Is that possible? Does that really exist? Oh, how we
longed for that experience, in the way he described it. Dr.
Aldrich was the President of Multnomah School of the Bible
in Portland, Oregon. We never heard of it.

Where is Portland, Oregon? Is it further west than Texas?

The conference was designed so several people could stay in each conference house. The speakers rotated, had meals and conversations in each conference house. We were eager to ask Dr. Aldrich more about that school. It sounded like a whole new world, inviting, intriguing.

My raging battle intensified over wanting to go to school verses serving in the church. The whole thing crescendoed when I meet Neil Glass, a highly respected godly leader. I requested a few minutes to ask a question. I tried not to shake, hoping I could speak sensibly, calmly. It spilled out at once.

"Do you think it would *ever* be God's will for me—*a woman* –to go to college? To get more education? What if it meant less time serving in church?"

> "I can see that your heart is filled with this desire. God clearly is moving in your spirit about schooling. I affirm your desire. I encourage you to pursue college. No matter the challenges, if this is what God wants, he will go before you. May I pray for you—for God's Spirit to confirm his will and his timing, in ways only he can."

His answer broke a dam of tears stored up over my two-years of frustration and confusion. He assured me being a woman was not the issue. God had a plan for my life as much as he did for every man *and* every woman. And it is all right to care about myself – that is not selfish. That is how God designed each of us. Jesus wants *me*? Jesus *chose* me.

"I encourage you to pursue that desire wherever it leads you."

The impact of God's confirmation through that conversation, that the dreams and desires of my heart were legitimate, was profound. God's Spirit truly generated them. His words began to carry me forward.

Lord, thank you for the clear confirmation again today that this dream is legitimate. Thank you for the freedom this gives for us to be whole human beings with legitimate desires—desires that are of you and not selfish whims to be put down or ignored.

That day I clearly stated my two lifetime dreams:

1. Get a college degree
2. Become a good writer

Lord, I begin now praying and trusting you for these dreams *to be fulfilled.*

I had been trying to see the whole of my life. I so wanted to see the next ten-plus steps before I took step number one. Now I realize I cannot and will not be able to see the whole plan—God has chosen not to reveal it. Rather, I am to live each day in faith, relying on God's wisdom. One step at a time.

Years later I learned that if God had shown me the *full plan*—what was in the years ahead—I would have been too scared to move forward. I would have *never* taken the next step.

I also realized one path was not higher than another. One person teaching bible classes full-time was *not* on a higher level than a person being a full-time student or full-time secretary, engineer, president or whatever. God was revealing his perspective on life—against mine.

God revealed these thoughts as lies:

- I am not enough.
- Don't anticipate joy or fun because you will be disappointed every time.
- We want you to meet our expectations.
- We don't want you. We would be better off without you.

God gave me these truths:

✓ Jesus is enough.

"My grace is sufficient for you, for my power is made perfect in weakness. Therefore I will boast all the more gladly about my weaknesses, so that Christ's power may rest on me. … For when I am weak, then I am strong." (2 Corinthians 12:9, 10c)

✓ Jesus brings real/full joy.

"As the Father has loved me, so have I loved you. Now remain in my love. If you keep my commands, you will remain in my love, just as I have kept my Father's commands and remain in his love. I have told you this so that my joy may be in you and that your joy may be complete." (John 15:9-11)

✓ Jesus through his Holy Spirit will speak to your expectations.

"I chose you and appointed you so that you might go and bear fruit—fruit that will last—so that whatever you ask in my name the Father will give you." (John 15:16)

✓ Jesus wants me!

"As the Father has loved me, so have I loved you." (John 15:9)

"I chose you and appointed you so that you might go and bear fruit—fruit that will last—so that whatever you ask in my name the Father will give you." (John 15:16)

"I took you from the ends of the earth ... I called you. ... I have chosen you..."

(Isaiah 41:9)

Lord, you simply want me to take the next step, to see the possibilities and step into the opportunity in front of me. *Chosen, God's dearly loved.*

--- *Excited?* Yes!

Chapter 16

No Cockroaches or Alligators

No cockroaches, poisonous snakes, alligators, or hurricanes?

Are you talking about heaven?

It is beyond Texas. It is on the left coast.

Portland, Oregon.

Our May 1984 trip home from the Chicago conference was anything but silent. Our thoughts, dreams, desires, possibilities and yes, opportunities flooded the atmosphere of our car and hotel room. Jim and I both felt a deep need for training. There really was a school that could teach us to do what we had both been trying to figure out for years? *Did we have the courage, the cost, and the determination to pursue it?*

The churches we served taught that schooling for ministry was not needed. More emphatically, it was undesirable. Each person was simply supposed to read the Bible, study the church commentaries, and repeat.

We discovered ministry was so much bigger. Both Jim and I felt a desperate need for more training, to be more effective in ministry – wherever and whatever that ministry would be.

Could I go to school and be glad about it? *How freeing that would be.*

Dr. Aldrich told Jim that he would likely get some credit

toward a degree for his years as a pastor. Jim had yet to complete his college degree. Jim's desire to attend Multnomah School of the Bible (MSB) was growing every hour, every day.

MSB was where? Portland, Oregon? *Where was that?* Texas was "out west," right?

Get out a map.

—

Once we returned home, we sent MSB partial applications and transcripts for academic evaluations. Meantime, we began thinking it would take at least a year to make such a huge life change. So, we started secretly counting the months until June 1985.

What were we thinking? We had two young teens to consider. What a surprise it would be to them, to our family, and to the church itself. That would be a *huge* move—from everything familiar (most of my life) to everything unfamiliar. I had never been west of Texas. Florida was summer all year long. Granted, I could do without the ants, roaches, poisonous snakes, alligators, humidity, thunder and lightning, hurricanes… oh well. *I wondered what Oregon had to offer.*

A month later we went on vacation with Lorraine and Dan to a cabin in North Carolina. It was an exciting time of relaxation, engaging with our soon-to-be tenth and eighth graders. We slowly began talking about our dream of getting more schooling. We told them about the conference and a school that was, yes, *in Portland, Oregon.*

We pulled out a map and had fun imagining some place that far from home. Predictably, Lorraine was ready to move. Dan, umm not so much. As they began to see we might be serious about this radical idea, they realized leaving their friends and changing schools would be—well, distressing. We tried to get them thinking of new possibilities out there -- new to us too, yet potentially exciting.

We arrived home a day early because we drove straight through.

That evening a call came from Dick Clark *in Portland, Oregon!*

Much to our surprise, he was not from MBS nor knew anything about our desire to go there. He was an elder in a church in Portland that was looking for their first "full-time worker" (pastor). Would Jim consider it?

How did he get our names? We had not even heard of him.

Dick Clark was on a board with Neil Glass and others at the Chicago conference. He called Neil asking for recommendations. Neil recommended us. By the questions he asked Jim, they seemed to be a more progressive church. We wondered if it would be like the ones Dr. Aldrich described.

Jim shared his view on some of the church's traditions that were simply not meeting people's needs. Dick said they understood and wanted none of those either. *In fact, Dick said it sounded like Jim was just the guy for whom they were looking.*

Jim shared his desire to go to school and Dick said that was great. They would work out the details. The church felt they were on the crest of new things happening.

It all seemed so surreal, that "out of the blue" this man called from *Portland, Oregon.* The elders out there discussed it that Thursday night. Friday evening Dick called back to ask if Jim would fly out next Friday (July 13) and stay until Monday.

Are you kidding? Next week?

Lord, this is all so unbelievable. Only you could arrange such plans.

Jim made reservations. He was trying to figure out a way to keep this all quiet—because it might never come to reality. If it did, who knows how long it would be before we could make the move. At least a full year, I imagined.

—

The next week would be the longest week of my life. Sometimes all the excitement inside just wanted to jump and scream. "We're moving!" But I had to keep silent until we knew the results of the interview.

If they wanted us, would they want us to move before June 1985? That would leave August 1984 or December 1984 as moving possibilities. Because we really did not want to move the kids in the middle of the school year, nor did we want to travel the 3,000 miles in a U-Haul truck with the possibility of blizzards, snow, or ice, that left August 1984 –less than two months. That was only five weeks away.

Impossible. Lord, that would have to be a first-class miracle to have our house and cars sold, plus a million other details, completed by then.

All things are possible with God—right. *Including this?*

How would the folks at our church react to such a quick move? Time helps people to accept new ideas—there would be no time.

Jim told an elder in confidence about the possibility of a move because Jim had to get Sunday free to go to Portland. The elder, true to his temperament, had no visible reaction emotionally. He said their church had no claim on us and it certainly appeared God had something in mind for us in Portland. *Whew...*

Thoughts constantly pervaded my mind. *If* we were moving in August, what could I do *now* to facilitate that move? Sleep failed in those moments of pondering.

Nights seemed long. If we only knew.

And frankly, we felt like the Holy Spirit had already moved us away from here. We had poured all we had into the work here. It produced fruit; we felt our time was up. No regrets. *Lord, we did all we could with your Spirit's enabling and we thank you for that.*

The possibility of gaining exposure, insights, and *yes,* even skills, in the areas of women's ministries, journalism, and Christian education was *exciting.* Could I take college minors in all those areas? All three interested me. *Lord, do you really think I could go to Multnomah too and get a degree?*

What a dream-come-true that would be for Jim too. What a release the day when he expressed his feelings of being cheated of an education by respected counsel in the past. What joy to express his desire to get a master's degree. *Lord, enable him to fulfill his dream too.*

—

Friday, July 13, 1984, Jim flew to Portland, Oregon.

The previous night was a short night of sleep. Anxiety juices were flowing freely.

In a matter of days our future "fate" could be determined.

Lord, give Jim safety and peace in you about the future. Open all the doors for us—give us wisdom in every decision. The hours seemed to drag by. It was Saturday, nine a.m. in Florida, but only six a.m.in Portland. Jim was probably awake but still in bed.

I felt like I was in the waiting room of life. Had surgery been performed yet? Was the surgery a success? Would we move to Portland? Or not? Would we move in four *weeks,* four *months,* or in a *year*? Or *not*? There was a significant difference, you know.

Sunday morning.

Jim called last night to say he had a gorgeous flight. The fir trees and forests were lovely there. He had breakfast with seventeen men --deacons and elders-- and shared his heart about the church. In the afternoon he was going to a barbeque at someone's cabin at Mt. Hood. One elder there was on the board of Multnomah Bible School, so they had already planned to take Jim to the school Monday morning.

Monday morning, I was in high gear—really all weekend the adrenalin had been flowing. I woke up wanting to jump up out of bed, as the thought shocked me, *again.*

We may be moving to Oregon in *weeks*!

We anxiously awaited Jim's phone call.

No call.

Lorraine and I both were getting real "antsy." I did some aerobics, sat down, and got sleepy. Lorraine fought it all night. I did not sleep well either. Tonight, Jim would be flying home. So hopefully we will know something then. My adrenalin gland must be stuck on *on*—hope it does not wear out.

As I suspected, Jim came home *without* a definite invitation. Waiting for the men in Portland to meet, decide and phone us.... All the information we gained about schools, weather, nature, et cetera, seemed inviting. Everything looked positive, but we were still on hold. Last night we talked 'til one a.m. and still the "antsy" was not gone.

When will we know? *How much longer can we wait, Lord?*

—

Lord, you must sustain me now—I have no strength of my

own left. When will they call? Did the delay mean things were in our favor—*or not?*

Finally, Saturday at ten p.m. Jim called one of the Portland elders to find out what was going on. He said the deacons had just met Saturday morning. The whole church was going to meet Sunday evening to make the final decision. So now, it would probably be Monday before we would get a call. Dare I hope for one late Sunday evening with the three-hour time difference?

It was refreshing to go to church and think about the Lord. But little darts of "what if" continued to fly by.

Sunday afternoon Alan Watford prayed a beautiful prayer in our behalf—knowing our anxieties. It brought tears to my eyes hearing him. Once a new Jesus follower, now ministering to us in our time of need. It really was uplifting.

I convinced myself they would not call from Portland tonight after their meeting—though Jim felt they might. It was hard to go to sleep—so we did not.

We talked, tossed, wondered, and tossed.

Chapter 17

The Landline Rang

The landline rang *at 10:47 p.m.*

Jim answered.

Dick Clark announced the church was inviting us to come to Portland

I thought Lorraine would be cheerleading, so I ran into her room and listened to her rah-rah in a loud whisper. Dan first seemed annoyed, awakened by all the raucous.

We all piled onto our bed listening for details.

After the short call, we learned that last Monday night after Jim left, the few elders that met, agreed he should come. Agreement followed in the Wednesday meeting and the Saturday morning meeting. And finally, agreement came in the Sunday meeting with the whole church.

But at eleven p.m., who could we call to tell?

So now, how do we sleep?

Lorraine and I agreed we did not feel like we thought we would when the big news came. The reality began to hit. She said she felt guilty because she wasn't sad about leaving but was excited. She did not want to leave her friends, but she felt like she was ready for a fresh start.

I shared that Jim and I felt that way at the beginning, but we knew when time for good-byes came, we would feel sad. I also told her when the opportunity to fulfill a dream comes (school for me), it would be worth taking the risk of many unknowns to pursue it.

Dan said he hoped he would wake up in the morning and it would all be a nightmare. He got his sleeping bag and camped out on our bedroom floor. *Hold him close, Lord.*

—

There was little sound sleep all night. At 5:30 a.m. we began whispering. At 6:30 a.m. we got up. Before long Jim called the local church elders.

Who would we tell first? How? What steps do you take when you need to sell a house in four weeks? *Lord, this will need to be another miracle. Please provide the realtor (if one is needed), the buyer and occupancy as soon as possible.*

Daily Vacation Bible School started that day. What a challenge in mind control. How would we ever carry on? Dan will want to tell his friend G. B. right away.

Once the dam leaked, there was no halting it.

Lil and I were at the table alone. I wanted to tell her before she heard it from someone else. She was shocked. In between registering kids, I began sharing the details. She finally said, "I must say, I'm glad for you if this is what the Lord wants, but it'll take time for me to handle my selfish desire for you to stay." What a dear sister in Christ.

It really was sad *and hard.*

The next hurdle was to tell my best friend Lois. After she finished with refreshments, I asked to talk to her alone. I could not bear telling this life-long friend. As the words choked out, I noticed she was not too shocked.

Then she said, "Bev, you won't believe this, but let me tell you what we've been thinking. We are planning to move too, to Tennessee." It was unreal how many of the same confused feelings we shared. It was almost a freeing thing to know they would be leaving too.

We continued sharing the news, with similar reactions. Glad, because it was obvious God had arranged the circumstances, but shock and sorrow over our leaving. It was hard leaving such lovely people.

Next, I would pick Mom up from the airport and tell my family.

Lord, thank you for the evidence of this week. You indeed have given Jim and me the desires of our hearts—the privilege of more schooling. Thank you. I know you are for me. Thank you, Lord, for so many good responses yesterday to the news of our move.

"By this I will know that God is for me." (Ps 56:9)

Mom took it quite well, though she expressed sadness that we would not be in Orlando—together with the rest of the family. Carole had no reaction or response, though she said she expected it from a few hints I had dropped. Paul said, "You lucky duck" and went on about how he would love to follow us out there. Palmer and Sue were not available yet.

We decided to give God a chance to work and sell the house without a realty fee. We put an ad in the newspaper and posted two fifty-nine-cent signs on the electric poles on the main road. If it did not sell within a week, then we would have to get a realtor. *Lord, we are all praying and watching for the miracle of a quick sale.*

One lady called wanting to rent the house. She had no down payment. She thought we were "bonkers" for thinking we would sell in a few weeks. There were lots of houses for sale in the neighborhood. *She did not know God was selling this house for us.*

Janice said she moved seven times in seventeen years of marriage. She encouraged me with tears in her eyes. "Bev, look ahead— let future possibilities excite you. Do not let the sad, 'sorry to see you go's' hinder you."

Then she said, "Though I *do* hate to see you go!"

I guess I wanted to hide from people's reactions because I did not want to face sadness nor regrets. I thought I was ready for new "vistas" and the sooner the better.

Delays only allowed more time for fears of the unknown to play havoc.

—

Dick Clark sent a "Prayer and Praise" paper. He included, "You may as well start being a part of the family. These should help." There was a prayer request for our move and adjustments as well. His wife Jeree called to say she was looking forward to making a new friend and wanted to help in any way she could. That made me feel like I would be going to at least one friend. It really made me feel "warm." What a gift—that one phone call!

We had no other requests to buy our house—except a realtor who called three times.

After I had crawled into bed, Lorraine came in crying. She said she did not want to go to a new school where she knew *no one*. She hated school as it was. Yes, she was tired, but the realities were beginning to penetrate. It would be hard, a teenager moving before starting tenth grade. Why had I not taken more time to process that pain? Would I ever become a good parent? How sad. How hard. I listened, hugged, and cried with her. Then I tucked her in.

I spent some time reading and praying specifics.

"The eyes of the Lord are on the righteous and his ears are attentive to their prayer..." (I Peter 3:12)

"The Lord is near. Do not be anxious about anything, but in every situation by prayer and petition, with thanksgiving, present your requests to God. And the peace of God, which transcends all understanding, will guard

your hearts and your minds in Christ Jesus."
(Philippians 4:5-7)

I thank you, Lord, for the new friends you will bring into our lives—especially for Dan and Lorraine. I thank you for the sale of the house in your time and for the price we will need to resettle in Oregon. Thank you for your peace just now in all the future unknowns. Please replace Dan and Lorraine's fear of the unknown with peace and security in you.

—

Sunday morning, Jim announced our leaving. There were tears—ours and others.

I began packing. As Mom and I were in my study packing books, a family came to look at the house. They simply saw the fifty-nine cent "For Sale" sign posted on the electric pole out on Hiawassee Road. The husband, D. L., taught at a local church academy. They really wanted the house. We prayed together before they left.

Thoughts flooded my mind that D. L. seemed the perfect buyer. He was a Christian and someone our neighbors would probably like. However, after discussing the details of the proposed contract, then going over to Hubert M. CPA for consultation, we were told it was not doable. *Lord, we must have your wisdom. We are not holding out for more money, but Lord, we just want to be good stewards.*

So, we went to bed assuming this was not God's buyer.

D. L. called and asked if he came up with a second mortgage, could he buy it?

We said, "Yes!" So, he began looking for one. *Lord, if it is D. L., then please supply the money he needs for a second mortgage.*

—

I looked out onto the Atlantic Ocean – perhaps for the last time. We were in a hotel suite at Cocoa Beach, a few moments from wedding time of dear friends. Their parents got us this room. At first it seemed like an interruption in the crucial packing and selling of our home. But soon we realized we desperately needed the break and rest.

Looking at the white webbed waves roll in seemed as unreal as the move ahead of us. The surprise of such a lovely site was a wonderful way to celebrate the signing of papers with D. L. at the mortgage company on our way over here. Did we really sell the house? *Yes, God did it!*

The move to Oregon would be the beginning of a new life – a new season.

Everyone marveled with us at the church in Florida *and* at the church in Oregon.

Jesus through the Holy Spirit is enough.

—

As I sat in our empty house minutes before starting our trek across the United States, to Oregon, I could not hold back the tears. The Imperials' song on the radio would leave a permanent memory.

> He didn't bring us this far to leave us
>
> He didn't teach us to swim to let us drown,
>
> He didn't build a home in us to move away
>
> He didn't lift us up to let us down. 1

We praise you Lord for selling our house seven days after we put two fifty-nine cent signs up on Hiawassee Rd! *Only God.*

As we packed the car, we said goodbye to each of the neighbors standing in our court.

As I gave one final glance at the empty house, tears were surfacing. I held them back as we pulled out. The Hislop caravan: a twenty-four-foot Hertz truck pulling a boat, with Jim and Dan inside the truck. Followed by the Datsun 210 with Bev and Lorraine inside, jammed full – roof rack and all.

As we pulled out, Dan's dear friend, G. B., ran alongside the truck waving good-bye to his best friend. Lorraine's friends were beside the car waving good-bye, as were the neighbors.

And on our car radio, at that moment, *guess what song played?*

> He didn't bring us this far to leave us
>
> He didn't teach us to swim to let us drown,
>
> He didn't build a home in us to move away
>
> He didn't lift us up to let us down. 2

YES, right then as we were pulling out of the court, the Imperials' song. *Again.*

The tears flowed freely.

Chapter 18

No Umbrellas Here

Our family, the four of us, rode all the way to the west coast. First time.

I loved the east coast—the beach in Florida was one of my favorite places. Feet in the warm, soft sand, the sunshine on the warm water. What was there not to love about the beach?

West coast, Oregon. We pulled up and parked on the ridge, Pacific Ocean. It looked similar to the Atlantic Ocean. The rocks and high ridge along the water were a new sight. We ran down to the water—all four of us. We walked along the waterfront in our clothes to decide if it was warm enough to get bathing suits on.

Minutes later, it started to rain.

What? Rain? We did not even think to bring our umbrellas down with us.

We all ran as fast as we could back to the car. *Whew... we made it.*

We sat inside looking out onto the beach realizing *no one* was moving. *Everyone* stayed on the beach just as they were. Some walking, some sitting. *No umbrellas.*

We were "newbies" and we had lots to learn about the Northwest, about Oregon.

If you used an umbrella, it was obvious you were from somewhere else.

—

Was I seeing a movie? Was this real?

As we approached the Columbia Gorge along the Columbia River for the first time, I was breathless. The beauty: pristine and colorful. Deep blue river surrounded on each side by rocky cliffs, mountains, trees, and lots of greenery. The 620 feet Multnomah Falls was breath-taking. I had never seen anything like that in my life. Were we in paradise?

Dick and Jeree Clark, and Mary Dryden met us in the Gorge, at Hood River, with warm hugs. They welcomed us to Portland. After lunch, the guys rode in the truck, the women in the car. Admittedly I had difficulty staying on topic with the conversation.

My eyes could not believe what I was seeing. "Does this ever become commonplace? Do you ever take it for granted?"

"It is beautiful, isn't it?" They agreed.

These dear women were so gracious. Over the next couple of hours, as we drove up the Gorge, they began telling me about the ministries for women at church. Once a week, older women gather and once a week younger women gather …

"How do you want to be involved, Bev?"

I was in too much of a daze to comprehend what they were asking, let alone respond.

I was in paradise now.

Later we would see if *I am enough* for this new world.

—

My first question in Florida when I met someone new was, "Where are you from?" And the answer was always another state, typically a northern state.

The answer I got in Portland was, "I was born on fifty-second street and now I live on 181st." *What?* Many grew up here – multiple generations, I learned.

As time went on, I worked to change my "y'all" into "you all." And eventually simply, "you." I wanted to be accepted in this part of the country. It was not easy for me. It was a different culture. It was one I began to love *–slowly.*

—

I loved making new friends. Two of the first to reach out to me, Jeree and Sharon, asked me to join them walking a two-mile trail around Glendoveer Golf Club three mornings a week.

"Good morning, Bev. How was your yesterday?"

"It was great. I had a chance to work in the yard—which I love. There were so many gorgeous roses, rhododendrons, and lilacs. But while I was on my knees clearing some weeds, a snake came out. I was surprised. But the shovel was nearby, and I was able to chop it up quickly. No injuries."

Jeree and Sharon laughed.

"What's so funny?" I asked.

"Why did you chop it up? We do not have poisonous snakes here."

What? How can that be? "What do you mean, no poisonous snakes here?"

"None here. I think there was a species in southeastern Oregon. But not west of the Cascades. Not here for sure."

—

We typically invited people over for Thanksgiving. As we began asking those in our new-to-us-church, we realized *everyone* had family close enough to gather with them. Can you imagine? Everyone. *What would we do?*

Dan was making friends in the neighborhood. John's parents invited us over for Thanksgiving dinner. What a joy that was for all of us. The Krieg family was so hospitable. It was a welcomed friendship. One we cherish to this day.

—

Christmas Day. We wanted to do something on Christmas Day we could not have done in Florida. We quickly opened presents and then drove up to Mt. Hood. It was covered with snow. What fun, snow skiing for hours. A new experience for me, Dan, and Lorraine. Jim of course spent years in Canada and was a natural at it. It became a new tradition for our family.

—

Dan made friends quickly at Parkrose Middle School and

in our neighborhood, friendships that continued through high school. Lorraine made friends from church, which meant they went to a different school than Parkrose High School. Lorraine's first year in tenth grade at Parkrose, brought tears nearly every day. Tears came to our eyes when she told us she went into a bathroom stall to eat her lunch. No room for her at the table.

—

I remembered the feelings I had that first night driving across the U.S. on our move from Florida to Oregon. In that motel room I journaled.

> This is our first night without a home, without an address, without a phone number (no cell phones back then). We do not even have money in a bank. We simply have a check from the house sale packed away. If we crash and die on the road, who will know?

A whole new experience.

—

Life experiences are lessons that last.

Textbooks? Not so much.

After multiple tries, I finally got an appointment with the registrar at Multnomah School of the Bible (MSB). Given a lifetime collection of courses from various schools, I was advised to go to Warner Pacific College (WPC) first. They would likely accept previous credits, leaving only eighteen for a bachelor's degree (BA). Then I could go on to MSB and get a Masters in Women's Ministries.

What? *Really?* I never dreamed of anything beyond a BA.

—

I was obviously much older than the students in the WPC class. The class registration form provided boxes to check for your age—but only up to twenty-four.

Not even close.

I started with literature courses. We were required to read lots of fiction, classic novels. Growing up we were told it was not good to read fiction. Only truth was worth reading. Reading a new genre was exciting. Each student gave a presentation of an assigned book. Mine was given last. *You are not enough* tried to intimidate me as I stood up.

Afterwards, Professor Stein told me my presentation was the best. For twenty minutes he talked about it. *What? Cannot be. Was I hearing correctly?*

> "Bev, you were so articulate. You drew us in. We were so intrigued. You made the characters come alive. You have such insight. You were well organized. Have you ever thought about writing? You seemed excited. Comfortable. You have a valued objectivity. I think you would make a good teacher."

Oh my! Jesus really is enough.

Life experience. The power of encouragement. I would never forget the impact, the time the professor took to speak such powerful words. Words that said to me, *Jesus in me is enough.*

For several days I woke up feeling wonderful. The grades? No. The text? No. Life experience.

I completed my BA in English.

Rain down on me Holy Spirit.

——

I wanted to fully embrace every word in my first MSB class. I was so excited.

"What do you need this stuff for?" On the way out of class a young student said she wanted to quit the course. I think she asked me because I asked so many questions in class. I just started leading a team of women and needed insights. The instructor had experience.

"It is helpful in ministry."

"Really? Do you actually use it?" She asked.

"Yes."

——

Next term in another class I had similar questions. "What do I need this stuff for? Will I ever use it? Should I continue in this class?" The male students verbally assured all of us that leadership was for men only.

Lord, I am struggling now with the time spent in this class. Should I continue?

I was not used to God answering me on the spot. I did not expect an answer. Yet I could not ignore the words I heard in my head. They were God's.

"Bev, someday you will be teaching a class like this one."

What? Only you God could ever *make that happen.*

"Pay attention to the style of teaching as well as the material."

I finally began taking classes in specific areas of ministry. I wanted to glean everything I could. The highlight was taking classes from Dr. Pam Reeve. Yes, a woman with her doctorate! She also had a counseling background.

Other students were involved in ministry or planned to be full time. They seemed to already know everything. Surely Dr. Reeve could see that this older woman was needy.

First, I was a woman. Yet I did not pour Kool-Aid or wipe little noses in church, as I was taught women should do. Was there really a place for me? A place to minister? It seemed other students were doing that. They had paid positions in their churches. Imagine that!

Secondly, would there ever be a place for a shy, introverted female?

A farmer's daughter?

Where did this idea come from—*that I could?* How did Dr. Reeve get to where she was?

I asked her.

She suggested we meet for lunch. We did.

Intimidation quickly dissolved as she reached out to me. It was not one word or one sentence. It was not just reading one more textbook. It was her presence. She believed in me, it seemed. As time went on, she proved to be a true mentor. A new life experience for me.

I was quiet in class. I was shy. I was still wrestling with thoughts of *we would be better off without you. I am not enough.*

Dr. Reeve broke through that lie. She shared some of her own uncertainties, challenges and yes, lies she believed about herself. As God began to counter the lies with the truth, Dr. Reeve chose to embrace the truth.

Now --- I had to. To counter a lie every time it surfaced, with the truth.

Jesus through his Holy Spirit is *enough. You are better off* with *him.*

———

Bobbi was a truly kind neighbor. She and her husband had two young children. When she found out we were involved in church, she asked if she could come. What a surprise! She came.

I asked if we could meet that week for lunch in a small local restaurant. We did. Near the end of lunch, I asked how she felt about church. She burst into tears and as her words carried her deeper, I asked if she wanted to ask Jesus to come into her heart, her life.

She did *not* say, "Yes."

Instead, she began praying right there at the lunch table—aloud—asking Jesus to forgive her sins and become her Savior! *Whew* ... Even though I prayed this would happen, I confess I did not expect it ... *right then* ... *right there.* What a precious moment. Bobbi began living out her new relationship. Others could see. Others joined her.

Jesus through his Holy Spirit is *enough. You are better off* with *Him.*

Umbrellas may not have been seen in Oregon, but God's Spirit clearly was. *Oh Lord, thank you for bringing us here!* The transition has been challenging on lots of levels. But today *I know that I know* you want us here. You chose me.

May your Holy Spirit pour down on us like rain.

Chapter 19

Manpower and Womanpower

Manpower Inc.

Multnomah School of the Bible.

Western Seminary.

Multnomah Press.

Doesn't anyone want to hire me? Our kids had both left for college—instant empty nest. Two college tuitions, plus living expenses.

I was ready for my first paying job. The challenge was completing the applications. I had plenty of experience all right. Just no salary numbers.

The Manpower Inc. interview seemed to go *very* well.

"We will get back to you."

No phone call. No one got back to me.

I went to MSB library two days in a row and saw the notice on the board for "Assistant Admissions." I thought I could meet the qualifications but was petrified about walking into the personnel office to ask about it.

So, I walked out to the car and left.

Both times I wondered if the fear was of you, Lord. But

I was not able or willing to pursue it. I also felt the pressure mounting to talk with Dr. Pam Reeve about the job.

After I got home, my emotions were telling me I needed to do something outside of church. I decided just to call and see if the MSB job was still open. The lady I needed to talk to, Irma, was not in. But Irma would return my call.

Irma did not.

Pam Reeve called. Not about the job. She simply asked me to share one session with the internship class, "How to Start a Women's Ministry." *Really?* Okay, yes. I will. Then she asked how I was doing. I told her I was looking for work. That was the seed I wanted to plant. She said she would let me know if she heard of anything.

Thank you, Lord for intervening. Now, I ask you to provide the job in your time that you have for me.

—

The Personnel Director at Western Seminary thought I might like the Faculty Secretary position, which was open. Only glitch? Jim was taking a class there. Not allowed.

Eventually she offered a half-time job, flexible hours, and good pay. Sounded perfect. The Director of Finance and the Personnel Director said everything but "you have the job." The Director of Finance said he did not anticipate anyone applying with experience in that area and was very willing to train me. A mere formality required that they posted the job next week. They would confirm I had the job on Monday by calling me.

Monday came. Monday went. No phone call.

I called Tuesday and learned many had applied. One woman had experience. She was being interviewed. A decision would be made by Wednesday morning.

I knew I would not get the job. I did not.

It was so disappointing because of the way the Lord seemed to lead in all the details—and the hours and pay were so ideal. Granted, I prayed during that week if this was not the job for me, the Lord would send along someone more qualified. Well, he did. I wrestled deeply with thinking the Lord had led me to apply for a job there. If I did not hear God prompt me to apply at Western Seminary, then I do not hear God at all. What are the implications of *that* in my life?

The Personnel Director said she had another job I might be interested in. A secretary to five bosses in a hallway in an attic. I left *not* wanting that job and I was thankful I did not get it.

The disappointment of losing the half-time position lingered.

It would be seven years before I understood.

God *did* lead me there.

———

I noticed an Editorial Secretary position at Multnomah Press (MP).

It was full time. *Could I do it?*

Jim encouraged me to apply. I had no emotion at all. I did

not want to get attached to the possibility of working there only to lose, *again.*

Thursday, I called. The job was still available. The Personnel Director was out until Monday. I picked up an application and worked on it.

Monday, I called. The receptionist said the Personnel Director would call me back to set up an appointment.

No call.

Why should she? She does not know me from Eve. Not womanpower.

I took my application in to the office at one o'clock. She agreed to see me on the spot! She interviewed me. She seemed excited. She asked if I could wait twenty minutes or so to see an editor.

I did.

I saw Liz and Al, the senior editors.

I was relaxed—not seriously thinking I would ever get this job. But if I did, I would need to regroup. It was full time.

I left MP detached emotionally. I still felt numb from the previous disappointment. MP said they would call me—*sure. Been there, done that.*

I was not counting on anything this time until it was for sure.

I followed recommendations to call the current secretary

and ask about the job. She was exceedingly kind and said they were trying to set up an interview tomorrow with all the editors.

They did!

I could not believe how lackadaisical I felt sitting at a round table with seven editors—four men and three women---interviewing me and introducing themselves. Totally relaxed. I left feeling and thinking I could be friends with this group of people.

I was a bit disappointed when Liz mentioned the pay range. I decided to go for the highest number--not caring a whole lot if they said, "Forget it."

They offered me the job. *Really?* At my requested pay.

I went in the next day for training. I had so much to learn. *Could I do this job?*

As the weeks went by, I began to realize how custom designed this job was for me. Unsolicited manuscripts were sent to me first. I had guidelines on what MP would publish and what they would reject. I informed authors.

A few weeks later Senior Editor Liz said, "Bev, you have a good eye for what we are looking for in a book. Your manuscript evaluations are 'right on!'" *Really?* I watched with great interest the editors' comments on the returned manuscripts I forwarded to them. They were each very affirming.

Liz asked if I would sit in on a "focus group" for Virtue

magazine on Monday. She had been asked but because of another commitment, she was not available.

Mike Hammel from Interest came in to see Liz. Afterwards, he talked with me about the book, *Resource Manual for Women's Ministry*. I had contributed several segments previously. It was the first book of its kind in that era. He wondered if perhaps I would use it in my class at MSB as a "test case." It would be great to have it published by then. Mike was meeting with editors at Victor Publishing next week. He would know more then.

Later Liz announced that the Editorial Department wanted to take me to lunch for Secretary's Day. We went to a Chinese Restaurant. They gave me a lovely card with some kind, affirming words. What a surprise. It felt so good.

Jesus through his Holy Spirit brings real/full joy. Yes, he does!

I loved working at MP. Eventually a big promotion came, and I moved offices, expanding my job opportunities. I learned more about the logistics of getting a book published. I met lots of authors. And participated in a national conference for MP authors, bestselling authors. They were real people, not scary stars.

Jesus through his Holy Spirit is *enough.*

———

Jack called from MSB and asked if I would teach a course in the spring. I could choose the subject and the time slot. I responded, "Yes." Then he said he would call right back to get that information.

A month passed. Two months. Three... no call.

Five months later he called.

Would I teach the course five months from now, in September? I agreed to teach the seven-week course, "Developing a Women's Ministry." He said there would be graduate and undergraduate students taking the course.

This was followed by more requests to teach at MSB.

—

Later I was asked if I would teach a session at the Red Lion MSB Women in Ministry Conference. "No. Thanks for asking. I do not see how I can just now."

I had such a full plate. I prayed *if this is of you, Lord, please show me.*

A few weeks later the leader of the conference, Barb, called and asked if I would reconsider my decision. She thought the *Women's Ministry Resource Manual* would be a great resource for the participants. She said I would only need to give eight to ten issues in women's ministry in a church of five hundred or less, then open it for questions.

Sounds simple enough, right?

"Yes, thank you, Barb. I will be glad to."

God, I believe you are showing me your will in this. Thank you for the assurance that when we do want your will, you will show it to us clearly. Now I can move ahead in full assurance that this is what you want me to do. And I trust you to bring it about.

God through his Holy Spirit will speak to your expectations.

> "I chose you and appointed you so that you
> might go and bear fruit—fruit that will last—
> so that whatever you ask in my name the Father
> will give you." (John 15:16).

———

Lyn Ludwick, a faculty at MSB, called. She asked if I would teach the final session of a class she had been teaching at Western Seminary. She was flying to meet President Bush, so would have to miss it. *Really?*

I said, "Yes."

What was I thinking?

I could not believe I said "yes" so quickly!

Lyn dropped off her briefcase at my house. She pulled out the class notes then said I could use anything else in her briefcase that I wanted. Frankly, I was too intimidated to even open it. I never even looked inside.

The class happened. Two hours. Teaching and discussion.

God answered my prayer. He gave me *his* words—in a powerful way. I enjoyed student engagement. It helped relieve my anxiety. A clean and empty vessel for God to speak through, my greatest desire.

It would be seven-plus years before I understood God's purpose in this teaching request.

Jesus through his Holy Spirit wants me.

Taken. *Chosen.*

Me? Yes, me. God's dearly loved.

Neither manpower nor womanpower.

Only God-power.

Chapter 20

I Do Not Have Time Now

"I do not have time now. I must get to class," I said.

Whew … I did it! Even though it was hard.

I never thought I could do it. It only took fifteen minutes.

—

She would say, "I disagree."

"I don't think that's a good idea."

"I wouldn't do it that way."

"Not for us."

On and on, for months now. She said it every time.

I heard, *we don't want you. We would be better off without you.*

Every time I led the church's women's ministry team in a discussion, she would interrupt.

The team was on board. The team brought great suggestions to the table. And we were ready to go with them. There was great support and excitement.

And then she spoke up. She looked directly at me. "That's not a good idea."

No one responded to her.

What should I do? I was taking a class on leadership. The text and the professor *both* said I needed to confront her. How could I ever do that? I had never done that!

I asked if I could drop by her house for a few minutes. She agreed.

"Good morning. Lovely home. Thanks for making time. I realize I am new at the church. I have so enjoyed getting to know everyone, especially the women on our team. I hope to get better acquainted with you and your family as well."

I sat down. I continued. "Each time I led the women's team, I went home conflicted. The conversation, the brainstorming, the planning all seemed to go well. And then your input stopped us. Like last week..."

I gave her several examples. I stopped. Fifteen minutes passed. I got up to leave.

"Don't I get to respond?" She asked.

"I am sorry, but I must get to class. I do not have time now," I said.

—

Conflict was hard for me. Typically, I ran from it. I did not confront it.

This time my professor encouraged me to confront her. Since I would be seeing my professor that day in class, I felt I must do the hard thing. I did. I confronted her. Then I hurried into class.

After class, my professor asked, "What did she say?"

"She wanted to say something, but I told her I had to get to class."

"And?"

"She asked if she could come to my house when I had time, and she could respond."

"And?"

"I hesitated, then said a quick, yes. But I don't think she will."

—

She did.

That day came too soon. I made sure I was home alone and had time. Would one hour be enough? Ugh… Not sure I could survive an hour.

She walked in with a confident look on her face.

"Bev, I have had a problem with you since the day you started coming to our church. Here are some of the reasons."

She pulled out a spiral notebook. Each page had twenty lines on it. Each line was filled, two and one-half pages! Each one was something I did or said. She took each one personally. She was offended at each one. She did not think I should be in any kind of leadership in her church.

We don't want you resounded in my head, *again.*

Oh God! Now what?

I asked if I could respond to each one as she read it.

She agreed.

"*Oh no.* What I meant was ..."

"*Oh my.* My question was intended to bring out suggestions from the team—including you."

I was shocked at how someone could take a comment, twist it, and internalize it differently than what was intended. Time after time. There must have been over fifty recorded in her notebook. As each one was read, I stated my intent. None close to her interpretation.

Oh God, please, please, please intervene! I do not know what is happening, but I so long for resolution. I hoped we could be friends. And now?

An hour passed. She finally paused.

I was emotionally spent. Couldn't she see?

We had twenty-five more to go! Tears began to surface.

There was silence.

"Bev, I guess the truth is I am jealous of you."

What? What did you just say?

"My husband and I hoped we would get the job you and Jim have here at church. We live here. We have been here most of our lives. You just moved from across the United States to be here. You do not know us. You do not know the Northwest like we do."

Shocked is too mild a word to describe me. I never, *never* expected that kind of response. *Did I say* never?

"Frankly, no one was more surprised than me when we knew God was calling us to come out to Portland, for this job."

"I know. It must be God's will. But I am having trouble accepting it."

"Would you do me a favor? Every time I say something that feels personally hurtful to you, would you let me know? Because I never want to hurt you! I never have. I need your help with this. Please tell me as quickly as you can. Then let us talk about it. Okay?"

"Okay. And I am sorry, Bev."

"I am sorry too. I am sorry I did not stay long enough last time to hear your responses. I never intended to cause you any kind of pain or frustration. I have lots to learn. I want to grow in friendship with you. You have lots to teach me. Please."

After she left, I began thinking of the awesomeness of forgiveness by another person.

Somehow, I know God forgives and that is astounding. But when another person feels you have deeply hurt her, she could easily seek revenge, harbor bitterness, smear your reputation, slander you, deeply hurt you. But when that person chooses to forgive you—genuinely—with no revenge or bitterness—that is awesome! *Godly.*

That was God in her. Only he could give the kind of spiritual strength to bring that about.

> "Whoever would foster love covers over an offense, but whoever repeats the matter separates close friends." (Proverbs 17:9)

*Hurt People, Hurt People.*₁ The insights in that book are strategic. But if all I remember is the title, well, that is life changing.

For me.

I will *make* time. Now.

Chapter 21

Introverts Do Not Speak

Introverts do not speak.

They hide.

They listen to internal voices. And sometimes external.

"Yes, it is Bev. What can I do for you?"

"Our committee decided we would like you to be our main speaker at the fall conference. You will have two sessions, morning and after lunch. Do you have room on your calendar?"

My calendar?

Me? Speak at your conference?

I must work twice as hard it seemed. I was not born with the skills. I felt intimidated. It was consistently a heavy responsibility. *Always.* No one else seemed to work that hard. It looked easy for them.

Taking the personality test emphasized *who I am.*

I began questioning why was I even involved in the church? I did not have the ability or skill set for it. Extroverts are the ones speaking at retreats, seminars, and conferences. *Right?*

When I was young, I was curious about "who am I." Now in mid-life, I knew who I was. I did not want to be reminded.

I wanted to focus on who Christ is and his beauty. Yes,

he is within me. *Jesus is enough.* Yet I worked on getting a "positive self-image." The more I found out about myself, the more desperate I felt a need for a "positive self-image." My personality alone was not enough.

But *God* could make something beautiful from my life! It was his Spirit in me that was the "positive image" I longed for. Taken. Chosen.

How utterly miraculous. Fantastic! That you, God, would dwell in me—knowing me. Couldn't you find a more gifted—a better person in whom to live? Yes, you surely could and that is what makes it even more awesome. *Bev,*

> You did not choose me, but I chose you and appointed you, so that you might go and bear fruit---fruit that will last … (John 15:16a)

That is remarkable Lord! And I have spent so much time spinning my wheels wondering if you wanted to use me, if you *could* use me. At that retreat? In that seminar? At that conference?

God, you obviously *chose me*—I had nothing or could have done nothing that would have attracted you to me—*you simply chose me!* My response was one of overwhelming gratitude and worship, overwhelming thanksgiving, Lord… *I want to become who you say I am,* your dearly loved daughter!

What can I do for you, Lord?

An introvert.

Speak at this conference?

> Lord, I have never been eloquent, neither in the
> past nor since you have spoken to your servant.
> I am slow of speech and tongue. (Exodus 4:10)

Moses' words reflected mine. Multiple times in my life. All four of Moses' responses to God, when asked to go speak, were mine.

1. Who am I that I should go? (3:11a)
2. Suppose I go, and they ask who sent you? What shall I tell them? (3:13)
3. What if they do not believe me or listen to me? (4:1a)
4. Lord, I have never been eloquent, neither in the past nor since you have spoken to your servant. I am slow of speech and tongue. The LORD said to him, "Who gave human beings their mouths? Who makes them deaf or mute? Who gives them sight or makes them blind? Is it not I, the LORD? Now go; and I will help you speak and will teach you what to say." (Exodus 4: 10-12)

Moses' response?

5. Pardon your servant, Lord. Please send someone else. (Exodus 4:13)

I *knew* I had to stop at number four. I *knew* I did not want to echo Moses' fifth response for the simple reason:

> Then the LORD's anger burned against Moses... (Exodus 4:14a)

I *knew* I did not want the Lord to be angry with me!

I lost count of the number of times I have returned to this text in Exodus.

> But Moses said to the Lord, "If the Israelites will not listen to me, why would Pharaoh listen to me, since I speak with faltering lips?" (Exodus 6:12)

Repeat.

> But Moses said to the Lord, "Since I speak with faltering lips, why would Pharaoh listen to me?" (Exodus 6:30)

It took Moses time to realize he did not need to be precisely articulate. It was not about his "faltering lips." The picture was bigger than that. He was simply the instrument through which God was speaking and working.

Oh Lord. I want to never forget, Jesus is enough.

God speaks even through introverts.

—

The next day as I was driving home from taking a MSB class, "Biblical Perspective on Women and Ministry," Jesus renewed his vision for me. He clearly revealed I would be teaching a class like this, in a college setting. *Really Lord?*

> Shall what is formed say to the one who formed it, "Why did you make me like this?" Does not the potter have the right to make out of the same

lump of clay some pottery for noble purposes
and some for common use? (Romans 9:20-21)

Thank you, Lord Jesus, for showing me *what kind of God
you are, Lord.*

Nothing is too difficult for you. Not even speaking through
an introvert.

Jesus through the Holy Spirit is enough.

Jesus through his Holy Spirit will speak to your expectations.

Jesus through his Holy Spirit will continue to speak when
you listen.

Taken. Chosen.

Being God's dearly loved.

Yes, even an introvert.

Chapter 22

Stay on the Couch

"Stay on the couch." That was the growing up message to myself.

My younger siblings went into the attic playhouse with our cousins.

The women were in deep conversation in the kitchen. The men, outside.

No one reached out to include me.

I made a lot of assumptions during those early visits back to family in Indiana. I was a pre-teenager. The memories resurfaced often.

I assumed they all agreed. *We would be better off without you.*

I thought if I did not cause any trouble, was quiet and simply stayed on the couch, I filled my role as the oldest child. Hide, Bev.

We don't want you and *You are not good enough* would also jump on board and join the already acclaimed *We'd be better off without you.*

I first heard those words as a six-year-old from that neighbor girl in Florida. They had maintained residence in my mind, heart and well, all of me.

My filter.

My interpretation.

My perspective.

I thought I should stay on the couch. Always.

—

But God!

Me, an introvert, yet *being God's dearly loved.*

I was sitting in a large church auditorium at an annual conference in Portland with hundreds of women. Ruth Conard was the main speaker.

Ruth Conard freely expressed the emotions she felt with each word. Powerful. Spirit-filled. She told us how God had "invaded her life" and sent the Holy Spirit in ways she would never have imagined. In fact, speaking was not something she ever imagined doing in life.

> But when the Holy Spirit enters and speaks to you, you know it is him and you know what he is saying. He has the power—you do not need to hunt for it, or think it is up to you. Simply open your heart, your mind, and your will, and ask him, "Fill me Holy Spirit. I open myself to *be* who you want me to *be* and out of that to *do* all you want me to *do.*"

All three hours I cried along with Ruth. I could not hide. I could not stop the tears. And I did not want to.

Lord, your Spirit is really zapping me again. "Thank you,

Lord. You again are renewing my vision to teach women. I still cry when I think of it. There is no doubt that is what you have for me. And I see being filled with your Spirit as the most important part of speaking."

Not just passing on facts.

Not trying to be perfect.

Lord, thank you for renewing that vision today.

At times I wondered if taking literature courses was removed from the goal of teaching women. It took so much time. Then I discovered the method for a character study in American Literature was like studying biblical characters. Maybe there was a benefit, a purpose.

Jesus is enough! Wow...

It was hard at first and very emotional to realize God really was saying that to me. I realized it was something my timid personality would never initiate—it had to be of him if it were to be.

"Lord, I am in tears again today thinking that you would choose to use me. To be a channel of your Spirit is my greatest desire in life. I am willing to make the sacrifice for this great privilege. Thank you for choosing me—most unworthy and undeserving, but willing and wanting more than any other desire in life, to be used by you. I love you, Lord. Here I am, send me."

I wanted to close the gap between who I believed I was—the

lies—and the truth, who God said I am. *Chosen.* God's dearly loved.

> You did not choose me, but I chose you and appointed you so that you might go and bear fruit – fruit that will last ... (John 15:16a)

It was the fuel I would need to proceed in Oregon, in the next season of life.

—

On the last day of the American Literature class, Dr. Erickson, Dean of Faculty, asked if I would like to work in the English lab. I could not figure out why she would ask *me* such a thing. *You want me?*

"What's involved?"

"Dr. Parker will give you the details. Here is her number."

After lots of self-talk and several fruitless attempts at calling, I walked into the library. Minutes later Dr. Parker came in. She seemed glad to see me.

"We need someone with your depth of English skills. I have done creative writing, but I have no depth of English grammar skills."

What did Dr. Erickson tell her?

Dr. Parker said the job was five to ten hours a week. I could work as many hours as I wanted. I would be paid every two weeks.

"We have no one with English skills like yours."

What? Me? Again, what did Dr. Erickson tell you?

"We really need you. Will you?"

"What is involved? Tell me more." I asked.

The job involved mentoring students needing assistance in English grammar skills.

I said "Yes."

After I got home the feeling overwhelmed me.

For the first time in my life somebody *needed* my skills?

Wanted my abilities? The Dean came *to me!*

The feeling overwhelmed me.

I reveled in it for three days. Somebody wants me!

"Hey world, somebody wants to pay me for an ability, a skill I have. Doesn't that make me a valuable person? *Somebody wants me!*"

Get off the couch.

As the school term ended, I realized this experience gave me a sense of accomplishment and fulfillment. I had the privilege of helping students.

Dr. Parker evaluated my work. "You always go the second mile with students. You are excellent in the way you communicate with each one. I hope you will come back next fall."

I have credibility beyond my home and church.

A first.

I was closing the gap between who I believed I was—lies—and the truth, who God said I am, *God's dearly loved.* Taken. Chosen.

May that truth become enfleshed in everything I think, say, and do, Lord.

Perhaps there was a world beyond the couch ...

Being God's Dearly Loved

Being God's dearly loved means letting the truth of our *being dearly loved* become enfleshed in everything we think, say, or do. It typically comes in four phases.

1. Taken 2. Chosen. 3. Broken. 4. Given

—

3. BROKEN

"Do not fear, for I am with you. Do not be dismayed, for I am your God."

(Isaiah 41:10)

I want to avoid, ignore, circumvent, or deny pain.

It is an unwelcome intrusion.

Pain confirms my negative feelings about myself. Pain hurts!

Will this pain break me? Then what?

Will God enter my brokenness?

Not Afraid? Not Discouraged? How can *that* be?

Is he really *with me?* What is *that* like?

Chapter 23

The Door Was Slightly Open

The door was slightly open. It was unlocked.

I locked it before I left. I know I did. Who opened it?

O God, help me!

"Hello. Anyone there?" No answer.

I slowly stepped inside. Gradually paced though each room. No sounds.

The window above the shower was shattered. Someone broke into the screened-in porch, then entered the house through the bathroom window.

O God, help me!

Fear began to engulf me. I ran back to the car and drove the fifteen minutes to Jim's office. He followed me back home.

We had just moved into a small house on seven acres in Palm Beach Gardens, Florida. Yes, moved again. This time from Portland, Oregon to south Florida. There was a single dirt driveway that ended at the house. The property was cleared. You could see our house from the overpass nearby and the apartments on the next property. There was no garage.

It was obvious. If a car was parked out front, someone was home. If there was no car, well, apparently that said, "Come on in."

No clues were found. We never knew who did it. We lost

valuable possessions. Too many to list. We had not completely unpacked yet.

More importantly, my feeling of safety was stolen.

The next morning when I went to the shower, I felt it. I was shaking. I did not want to shower. It would be okay if I smelled sweaty all day, right? Probably not. Remember, it is south Florida--always hot and humid.

O God, help me!

He did. God gave me a verse to repeat throughout the day, especially when I was in the shower.

> You, LORD, are a shield around me, my glory, the one who lifts my head high. I call out to the LORD, and he answers me … In peace, I will lie down and sleep. For you alone, LORD, make me dwell in safety (Ps 3:3-4a; 4:8).

I did not want to move from Oregon to Florida. We had moved from Florida to Oregon seven years prior. I was beginning to find myself in Oregon. *And now this.*

Jim was offered a pastoral job at a North Palm Beach church. Our daughter and son were both in colleges in California. I came back from visiting my family in Florida when Jim told me our Oregon house had sold. I hoped that would take longer.

God, how could this be? Do you *really* want us to move back to the state we came from---hot, humid, roaches, poisonous snakes, insects, alligators, lightning, and thunder?

I made a list of "pros and cons" on moving. Quickly two full pages of reasons *not* to move surfaced. In all fairness I knew I needed to start a page of "pros." There were only two.

1. Jim wants to.
2. I know God wants us to, *but God I do not want to.*

Soon a semi-truck dropped off a piggyback container and we spent a week filling it. A week later, it was picked up, put on a train, and sent ahead of us. We drove all the way to Palm Beach Gardens, Florida, in our pick-up with a camper on back.

A stop "on the way" was Hawaii, where we met both our daughter and son for a week together. It was a celebration of their high school graduations and beginning of college. We had a fabulous time together. I loved every minute. And keeping my mind on the beauty in front of me was a great diversion from what was yet to come.

I would grieve the loss of those memorable pictures taken in Hawaii, when our camera bag was stolen at that break-in. Pictures from Oregon where also lost. Never to be recovered.

—

It soon became clear that Jim had a seven-year cycle. A good word picture was that of a boat on the bottom of the water. Jim was called to bring that boat up out of the water, provide needed repairs and fresh sails. Then it would need someone else to "set sail" again.

We lived in Oregon seven years. Jim felt it was time to move on to another "ship." Sure enough, the call –unsolicited—came. Jim was ready to go.

The people in the church were so warm and accepting. They purchased seven acres with plans to build a larger building there. Meantime, the existing house on the property was used as a recovery home for young women. Just before our arrival they moved that ministry to another location. A whole new reality of stepping into enemy territory surfaced.

One I had never experienced.

I could never relax in that house. I would sit on the couch and try to pray or read. Eventually I would run outside, look up to the heavens, and begin to pray – for a brief time. But as soon as I went back into the house, the same feelings surfaced. I felt fear and silence from God. Why this house? The church was providing it, rent free.

"Lord, I am asking you to relieve me – to give me victory over the daily battles of fear of being in this house—of being robbed again. *Please!* Please give me the peace you promised in Philippians, which will keep me from constantly staring out the window to see if anyone is coming up the road."

> The Lord is near. Do not be anxious about anything, but in every situation by prayer and petition, with thanksgiving, present your requests to God. And the peace of God, which transcends all understanding will guard

your hearts and your minds in Christ Jesus.
(Philippians 4:5b-7)

The darkness in the house became even more obvious when I got into the car and drove to my family in Orlando. It was such a joy praying and praising the Lord in the car for the three-hour drive. As soon as I returned to the house, the darkness set in. Is that what spiritual warfare is?

On the way to the grocery store I cried out. "God, did you not get my forwarding address? Why am I not able to pray to you in that house? *Where are you?* Are you not here in South Florida?"

—

It was January. I drove to the local mall to meet a new friend for lunch. A short conversation came on the car radio. Two men were talking about Moody Bible Institute courses available in Boca Raton, Florida. A 1-800--phone number was given.

For the first time since we moved here, I felt God prompted me. "Call."

I did. The response was only an answering machine with more information. I hung up.

God what was that about?

"Bev, that is what I have for you."

What? Are you serious? How could that ever happen?

"God, if you are serious, you will have to make this happen.

I have no idea how this could ever happen in my lifetime, let alone now."

End of conversation.

I enjoyed the lunch with Joanne at the Gardens Mall. She was a treasured new friend.

—

January and February found me struggling to stay on the rim of the black spiral downward. I cried multiple times, *"My God, my God, why have you forsaken me?"*

My mind knew he was there, but my heart could not feel him. My eyes could not see him. My ears could not hear him. *Why did you bring me to South Florida, Lord? It feels dark here.*

The next morning, I found myself reading Jeremiah 29:4-12. I wondered if God was leading me to this text. I would not know until later.

> This is what the LORD Almighty, the God of Israel, says to all those I carried into exile from Jerusalem to Babylon: "Build houses and settle down; plant gardens and eat what they produce... Find wives for your sons and give your daughters in marriage, so that they too may have sons and daughters. Increase in number; do not decrease. Also seek the peace and prosperity of the city to which I have carried you into exile. Pray to the LORD for it, because

if it prospers, you too will prosper.… Do not let the prophets and diviners among you deceive you… I have not sent them … When seventy years are completed for Babylon, I will come to you and fulfill my good promise to bring you back to this place. For I know the plans I have for you, …. plans to prosper you and not to harm you, plans to give you hope and a future. Then you will call on me and come and pray to me and I will listen to you."

God are we in Babylon? How long will we be here? Jim has a seven-year cycle…*not seventy years.* I cried out to God. *I thirst for you God. My soul pants for you God.* God knew he finally had my full attention. In that darkness, I had nowhere to go but to Jesus.

Yet I could not hear his voice.

—

Sandy was an amazing woman on multiple levels. *Every time* I saw her, she exclaimed,

"Bev, guess what God did?"

"Bev, guess what God did?"

"Bev, guess what God did?"

Yes, I mean *every time* I saw her. And clearly God was speaking to her, leading her, and doing incredible things in her life. Her back story was frightening. Her current story was

158

miraculous. I knew her God was the one I wanted to know better.

"God why are you always speaking to Sandy—always doing things in her life—and not in mine?" I fell on our couch and began crying.

"Bev, I *am* speaking to you, but you are not listening. I want to do things in your life too, but you are not looking for me."

"Lord, I know I am useless, worthless, not wanted. I know I am not enough. I know everyone would be better off without me. No one wants me. I cannot meet anyone's expectations. How could I ever meet yours, Lord? *I cannot.*"

Broken.

Instead of denying my brokenness, I stepped into it.

I acknowledged it.

I did not expect to come out alive, that is, in Jesus's eyes. I tried to believe the truth, but the lies continued to resurface. I expected the lies I had believed my whole life about myself were now going to be confirmed by Jesus. He could cast me out forever. And the darkness and distance I had been feeling would be that and more, the rest of my life. I deserved it. *How could he love me?*

I heard God *in that house* for the first time. He broke through. His words changed my life forever.

"Bev, your sin may not be obvious to many. But it is the sin exposed over and over in the Pharisees. You care more about what people think of you, wanting to meet their expectations. I want to expose it in you. Until you see how sinful your heart really is, you cannot *fully* know my love, forgiveness, and grace. I have wanted to do things in your life, but you would not let me. You were not open to my words. You stayed hidden. You wanted to lead your life. You judged others and me, like a Pharisee."

Tears flowed. I was on my knees on the floor. I felt the floor might break open and I would fall into a cave—never to be seen again. I had never felt God's presence so powerful before that moment.

"Oh God, I am so sorry. Please forgive me. I do not want to be like a Pharisee. I want to love like you love. Show me how."

The biggest surprise of my life followed.

I felt God's love at that moment in a way I had never felt it before. All the lies I believed about not being enough were overcome with God's genuine love for me. It was as if he was putting his arms around me and holding me close to his heart. No words could fully describe …

I remembered what Jesus said about the Pharisees in the Bible. Seven times Jesus said,

"Woe to you, teachers…you hypocrites … blind guides…" and worse. (Matthew 23:13-39)

You clean the outside of the cup and dish, but inside they are full of greed and self-indulgence. Blind Pharisee! First clean the inside of the cup and dish and then the outside also will be clean. (Matthew 23:25-26).

My life had focused mostly on "the outside." I wanted to appear to be a good girl. I did not want to create any conflict, adversity, disobedience. I wanted to be liked by everybody. *Isn't that how you do it?* Just be a "good girl." Protect yourself. Hide. Sit quietly on the couch.

I had not honestly looked closely at the "inside… full of greed and self-indulgence." Yes.

Broken.

If you were to ask, 'step forward the worst of sinners,' it would be *me.* Some of the harshest things that were said about the Pharisees, were true about me.

Broken.

How could he love *me?*

Love—unconditional love flooded my being.

Your love, Jesus, surrounds me—I see it, hear it, and yes, I even feel it—to a level I have never experienced before. To the level that says there is no sin worse than mine yet forgiven. Jesus through the Holy Spirit declared, *"I love you as much now as I ever have and ever will. I chose you to be my daughter.* You are chosen. *I have a plan for your life—designed before you were born--to serve and glorify me."*

TAKEN, CHOSEN, BROKEN... *God's dearly loved.* That truth deepened.

How can that be? I am a sinner—forgiven *and* dearly loved.

God said to me, "I will do things through you that you never imagined or dreamed of. I will go beyond your fears, inadequacies, and weaknesses. You will always be aware of me doing it through you."

If Jesus could love me, he could love you—anyone and everyone. And he does! He gave his life—the cruelest of deaths on a cross —because he loves me *and you!*

On December 13, 1992, the supernatural invaded the natural. Jesus Christ, through his precious Holy Spirit touched me in a way I had never been touched before.

Moments later I remember saying, "Lord, if you put me on a shelf the rest of my life, that is not only okay, it is good. Because I know you will be right there with me on that shelf *loving me. And that is all that matters!"*

I honestly thought I would never be asked to teach or talk about God again. I did not deserve to. Now it did not matter. I was content. Because I felt God's love for me every minute, hour, day ….

And that is all that mattered.

Forever.

Sandy, guess what God did?

…. The door was about to open wider.

Chapter 24

The Door is Wide Open

Same house.

Different door.

God opened this one. Just for me.

It was January. We had been in this house for one year.

The Florida Moody Bible Institute (MBI) Extension Classes Coordinator requested breakfast with Jim and me, to meet the new pastor in town. Paul Kangas told us about MBI courses available in Florida.

The Spirit of God nudged me. *Remember Bev what I told you one year ago today?*

I wondered if Paul would know ...

I finished my breakfast. My plate was empty. Paul asked what I had done in churches before moving here. A few sentences later, he could not say it fast enough.

"Bev, we would love to have you teach a class this spring *and* develop a Women's Ministry package for MBI. And if you are willing you can teach all over the state where MBI classes are taught."

Lord, you are Almighty, faithful through the ages. You have had your hand on me all along...all the way to south Florida. I thank you Lord. And you have prepared me. Now, Lord, I am trusting you to give me the material to teach—the what and the how. It is up to you to draw your choice women to these classes—specifically the Women's Ministry track.

A month later Paul went over all the details. He would line up the first class on Spiritual Gifts in March at the Boca Raton site.

—

As I drove nearly an hour to the first class, I continued praying. "God, you know there needs to be at least ten students to have a class. Since there is no pre-registration, I will not know until they walk in at the beginning of the first class. If there are not ten, the class must be cancelled. Yes cancelled, after preparing for an entire course. *Your will, Lord!"*

After I finished setting up, a couple of students walked in. Then a couple more... As I looked up at the clock, I realized it was time to start. I could hardly believe the count. There were twenty-one students. *Lord, you sent double plus one. What an unspeakable joy!*

As I stood at the front of the classroom, I realized a life-long dream was coming true. This was what I was born to do. To teach adults in a classroom setting.

I loved being with these women. I loved their responses and interaction. I loved their input and the thrill of seeing "lights come on." I loved seeing the Lord speak to them personally. The Lord revealed students' spiritual gifting and began changing the struggles many of them had with trying to fit into someone else's mold. *Praise you, Lord!* "A newfound freedom," several said.

—

Prior to the next term, WRMB Radio asked me to do a five-minute live interview over the phone, to promote the next course.

Really Lord? I had never done that.

I was so nervous. Scared really. What if I said something silly ... or worse? It was *live!* I could not see anyone; it was over the phone.

I got up early that morning—incredibly early. I could not sleep. The interview was seven a.m. I did not drink coffee, but tea worked. I had asked a couple of friends to pray specifically for me—that I would be articulate and inviting. They prayed.

It happened. Five minutes.

At the end, off the air of course, the interviewer said, "Bev, that was really great! You were *articulate and inviting.* Thank you so much."

Only God could have brought those words out, mine and the interviewers.

Little did I know at the time, the next fall term Moody would ask me to come to the radio station for a one-hour *live* interview. That was one of the main ways to get the word out about the Women's Ministry Track. It would precede each term moving forward.

God, you continue stretching me beyond my comfort zone.

But if you continue to speak through me as you did this morning, I am willing. Only God could make this happen!

—

The leader of the national Decade of Promise Conferences called to ask if Carol Porter and I would do two pilot seminars in 1993—Women's Ministries in key U.S. cities. His team would plan and take reservations. If the responses were good, he wanted us to plan an extended women's track for 1994 and 1995, and possibly beyond. We accepted.

Carol Porter, a leader in ministry to women, had called a team of us together to write chapters in the new hardback, *Women's Ministry Handbook.* It was the first of its kind in that era. It was a joy meeting together with other women – all on the front lines of developing Women's Ministries in local churches and communities around the United States. What a comradeship we felt with each other. Our relations deepened as time went on. Even though each of us was starting something new in our local communities, it was great to know we were not alone. Others had similar visions.

That book still sits on my bookshelf, filled with memories of those early years.

Thank you, Lord, for the opportunities you gave.

Thank you for invading my life.

The invasion continued.

—

Panic. Anxiety. Stress.

How heavily they fell on me.

I could hardly breathe – or *think* about what else I could be doing.

My airfare to Denver was paid along with the workshop fees. Was I really going to do this?

Dynamic Communicators Workshop provided opportunity for men *and* women to prepare and give several five-minute speeches in a group setting. Input from each other plus a "professional" gave value to this learning experience.

God gave me my first speech in the middle of the night the week before. I discounted that speech several times and considered it my worse. *Yikes! Did I really agree to this?* What could be more intimidating? I was such a novice.

Okay God, you know I need this desperately. I am willing.

I was scared.

What? I was put in a group of all men! How did this happen? Triple the nerves.

Oh God, help! I know you are enough, Jesus. *Help me to stay focused on you, Lord, not on the men or myself.*

My turn. I stood up and … well, talked.

When I finished, I wanted to run. *Men! What will they say?*

One guy spoke up right away. All the others said they agreed with him.

"Send her home. She does not need to be here."

What? Did I hear him correctly?

I am not enough, *surfaced quickly.* Just when I thought that lie was gone forever. Are you guys agreeing with me? *I am so bad that there is no hope?*

"Send her home?"

God help me. I know you are enough, Jesus. .... *What now?*

The guy continued. "I have heard a guy who is paid half a million dollars to jet around speaking. Your five-minute talk on Fear was clearer and more powerful than anything I have heard him say. Bev, you should hit a speaking tour."

What? Did I hear him correctly?

"Bev, I have been trying to tell you. I, Jesus, through the Holy Spirit am enough. When will you get it? How about *now*?"

"Lord, I look to you and say, thanks! How gracious you are to meet me at the point of my greatest need. Again, you have confirmed, I can trust you. Forgive me for the enormous fear and anxiety I felt over this. You placed me in a group of all men—which at first, I wanted out. Then I realized I have had a fear of speaking in front of men. Perhaps this was your plan for me, that I should move through that fear too. So, I will stay in this group. Teach me, Lord."

"Bev, remember, you are God's dearly loved. Taken. Chosen.

—

Is there more?

Yes. Can you believe it?

The desire of my heart—my first magazine article published.

November 1992, "The Changing Moods of Moving." Interest magazine.

Sometime around 1980 I wrote as a long-term goal to have a magazine article published. Twelve years later, a degree in English and MA ...

Lord, we both know you *wrote it.* You woke me up at two a.m.—Jim and I were in a motel in Cocoa Beach, Florida—and you gave the article to me, nearly word for word.

Later, Carol Porter called and asked how I was doing. After I told her about our move, she said, "Why don't you put that in an article?" I sent it on to her. She said it was "excellent." She forwarded it to the editor, and I heard nothing. Months later, it appeared. Fifty dollars plus two free magazines came *after* it was published.

Again, Lord, you have your hand on my life in a remarkable way. How could I ever doubt? How could I ever dwell in a slump? You have given me above and beyond my wildest expectations!

Also published in Interest magazine:

"Prayer Power and Triplets," March 1993.

"Essential Ingredient" (Jesus, our first love), July/August 1994.

Lord, forgive me for wanting things my way—my comfort zone. I realize the challenge I need comes from you pushing me out of that comfort zone into new vistas for you.

You *do know* me. You *do* have your hand on my life.

You have revealed more of who I am. You have touched my uniqueness. You have purified and deepened the truth that *I am God's Dearly Loved.*

And happy 46th birthday, Bev...

The door is wide open.

Jesus is the door keeper.

Chapter 25

Supernatural Invades the Natural

On December 13, 1992, the supernatural invaded the natural.

Jesus Christ, through his precious Holy Spirit touched me in a way I had never experienced before. The Bible verse that enabled me to move from Portland to South Florida was

> Those of you who do not give up *everything* you
> have cannot be my disciples. (Luke 14:33)

At that moment I confessed the emotional attachment to Portland. *Oh, Lord, how your Spirit flooded my soul with his presence.* The Spirit gave me God's perspective—the "wonderful" things I did in Portland suddenly appeared as wood, hay, and stubble, compared to what God had been doing through me in Florida. It took removing all my joys, comforts, accomplishments, experiences, and life-time opportunities.

The severing felt complete, "… give up everything …"

> "Very truly I tell you, unless a kernel of wheat
> falls to the ground and dies, it remains only
> a single seed. But if it dies, it produces many
> seeds." (John 12:24)

The Holy Spirit gave me an overwhelming burden for Florida. He clearly said he wanted to reach the state of Florida through me—using prayer triplets. I was up at two-thirty a.m., and suddenly realized it was six a.m. Oh, how it felt like heaven, to be in God's presence. Hours passed like minutes. I wanted to stay forever.

Lord, I want my heart to remain pure and clean for you. I want you, Holy Spirit, to remain fully in me. I love you and my soul truly has found rest, peace, and ecstasy in you.

Taken, chosen, broken… I *am* God's dearly loved.

Pam Reeve said in June of that year, "It sounds like God has anointed you for the ministry he has for you, Bev." Perhaps that prophesy was fulfilled on December 13, 1992. *Oh God, I have never felt so deeply in love with you. I really want to spend my days communing with you—just being in your presence.*

Each day I longed for more. I did not know how to explain this.

I began asking others, "How do you become filled with the Holy Spirit? How do you continually feel his presence?"

A special couple at church that loved God, "I don't know Bev."

A new friend who seemed godly, "I don't know Bev."

A church leader, "I don't know Bev."

No one I asked could answer my question.

Lord, don't you want all your followers to be filled with the Holy Spirit? Then please lead me to someone who can tell me how to not only initiate this, but to bring it *daily. Isn't that your will for us?*

—

Weeks later Jim and I went to a national conference, Decade of Promise, held in a school in Chicago. I was lifted into the heavenlies through the music and message. I was sure someone there could answer my question. But who? I searched through the lengthy list of seminars offered.

The closest I could find was called, "Recovering the Art of Christian Contemplation." A well-respected godly man led it. Surely, he would tell us. All the way through the seminar I could hardly wait to hear him answer my question. He did not. At the end, he asked if there were any questions. He only had time for three, he said. Out of the four hands that were raised, he chose the other three.

Then we were dismissed.

I walked up to him. As he shook my hand, I asked, "How do we bring God's Holy Spirit fully into our lives, forever?"

"I do not know. But I can clearly see he is in you."

Tears filled my eyes. I left that room. I walked out onto the sidewalk. I collapsed, sitting against a classroom wall. I cried out to God. I felt like I was at a dead end.

How could this be of you, Lord? No one seems to know how to be filled with your Holy Spirit. No one has the answer, God.

"That is your problem, Bev. You are always looking to people for the answers." At that moment, sitting on the cold sidewalk, the Lord clearly said, "Bev, remember the verses I gave you from Jeremiah?"

You will seek me and find me when you seek
me with all your heart. I will be found by you,
declares the Lord. (Jeremiah 29:13-14a)

"Bev, you have been seeking me with all your heart. The answers are not always from people. Come to me and ask me. Because when you seek me with all your heart, I will be found by you!"

1992 began as the darkest.

1992 ended as the brightest year ever.

The magnitude and beauty of 1993 was greatly anticipated.

…. The supernatural invading the natural.

Chapter 26

Only One Seat on This Flight

"I have only one seat left on this flight. Do you want it?"

"Yes!"

Seriously? *Oh Lord, what are you doing?*

"Bev, my name is Katherine. I have not met you, but I believe you should come to Chattanooga, TN, December 11-14 with us. We will be at Kay Arthur's place. Fifteen women, leaders of organizations and ministries from around the United States are invited. I called and it is okay if you join our group. Friday through Saturday Evelyn Christenson will teach us how to train others to pray in groups of three, using her new book *Pre-Evangelism Praying.* Sunday through Monday, we will be discussing how to implement her plan."

Who? Me? *Seriously?* Kay Arthur was an internationally known leader, as was Evelyn.

Katherine and I flew from Florida to Tennessee on the same plane without connecting. How would I recognize her? Where would I go after I got off the plane? *This was very strange.* Slowly I made my way up to the front of the plane. It was empty. I stepped outside. I looked around. A woman stopped me, "Are you Bev?" It was Katherine. *Relief.*

After settling into our hotel room, Katherine led me to the room where fifteen women were settled around a table. As the plan unfolded, my heart raced. I was nervous. *Me?* Around *this* table, with *these* women? The vision was to train women in each state to form multiple groups of three to pray specifically for women to come to know Jesus.

That was the beginning of the AD2000 Movement North American Women's Track 1992. Fresh off the press was *A Study Guide for Pre-Evangelism Praying.* "Ladies, how will you use the study guide and how many do you want? 100, 1,000 or more?" As Evelyn went around the table with these questions, most responded in high numbers. They were ready to get started. When it came to me, I hesitated … stumbled…

I cried out, *Lord, I do not even know why I am here. What do you have for me?*

Early the next morning God answered that cry in one of the clearest messages I had received from him.

"Bev, I want you to begin praying for the state of Florida by county. I want you to pray

1. Christians to be revived —to have a passion for Jesus.
2. Christians to pray in triplets for the lost souls—prepare and open spiritual eyes.
3. Triplets in every neighborhood, school, family, workplace—in every county."

FIN—Florida Intercessory Network was birthed. I began praying daily for each county in Florida—two per day almost equaled a month.

—

Nine months later as I was flying 30,000 feet above the United States, God gave me the names of five women from around Florida, to form a FIN team. Emilce, Gloria, Geri, Patricia, and Joanne. They all said, *yes.*

These women had never met before our first meeting together. I had only briefly met each of them. Their ethnic and denominational lines reflected the diversity of Florida. The Spirit of God moved the first time we met together. We bonded in an incredible way—each had a passion for God and a compassion for the lost. Our first meeting was extended several hours as we each transparently shared our stories and prayed together.

We asked God to show us the next step and make clear his objectives. God did.

Revival was initiated, walls were breaking down. Each of us used the Study Guide in seminars on triplet praying held in various counties and churches. The vision multiplied. Stories of God's work flooded in.

In February I asked the FIN team to pray and ask God if he wanted us to go to the annual AD2000 Conference in Wheaton, Illinois.

"But we have no money, Bev."

"Would you be willing just to pray?"

"Sure." They agreed. "God, we need $2400."

When we met on a Saturday in April, each woman said, "Yes, God's telling me he wants me to go, but I have no money."

Monday at seven a.m. a call came, "God told me to pay all the airfares for FIN."

She did. What a fabulous vision, enhanced even further at the conference. I wrote in my journal: "I never felt so sure about anything in my life. I love the feeling of being filled with the Holy Spirit, and teaching women to pray." This was the ultimate for me. *Dear Lord Jesus, please put a hedge of protection around me, that Satan will not penetrate with fear or lies.*

Jesus is enough. *Jesus is all I need!*

———

After returning home, I called the woman who led the live-in recovery ministry that was held in our house. I openly shared how I could not hear God when I was in that house. She quickly responded, "Of course not. You did not have someone pray through each room of the house before you moved in?" *What?* "One of the girls living there was from the streets of New York. She fought consistently with the enemy. We prayed for demonic expulsion multiple times when we lived in that house. Spiritual warfare was prevalent."

This was unfamiliar territory for me. It explained so many things in the last months. The Lord protected us day after day. He drew me to connect with him outside of that house. And then he finally broke through inside the house. *Lord, thank you for not giving up on me.*

The next morning, I found myself in Jeremiah chapter twenty-nine, *again*. This time I more fully embraced the words. They were indeed for me.

> This is what the LORD Almighty, the God of Israel, says to all those I carried into exile from Jerusalem to Babylon: "Build houses and settle down; plant gardens and eat what they produce... Find wives for your sons and give your daughters in marriage, so that they too may have sons and daughters. Increase in number; do not decrease. Also seek the peace and prosperity of the city to which I have carried you into exile. Pray to the LORD for it, because if it prospers, you too will prosper. Do not let the prophets and diviners among you deceive you... I have not sent them ... When seventy years are completed for Babylon, I will come to you and fulfill my good promise to bring you back to this place. For I know the plans I have for you ... plans to prosper you and not to harm you, plans to give you hope and a future. Then you will call on me and come and pray to me and I will listen to you." (Jeremiah 29:4-12)

We purchased property and began drawing plans to build a new house. Lorraine was beginning a serious relationship, as was Dan. Both would marry. We would indeed plant a garden on the property. I began to believe we were to settle in. It could be another seven years here. Sounded like that Scripture.

So, I started embracing God's "plans to prosper you and not to harm you, plans to give you hope and future." Yet another step was given.

> Then you will call on me and come and pray to me and I will listen to you. You will seek me and find me when you seek me with all your heart. *I will be found by you (italics added)*, declares the LORD, and I will bring you back from captivity …back to the place from which I carried you into exile. (Jeremiah 29:12-14)

We were indeed in exile.

But God was right here with us … in exile.

… That was the only seat on my life flight that mattered.

Chapter 27

Welcome Home, Finally

Welcome home, *finally*.

An amazing thing happened. I will try to put it into words.

I felt the day we left Portland that this move was two years premature—certainly for me emotionally. It had been an *exceedingly* difficult two years—the darkest times ever in my life. Yesterday was the beginning of our third year.

It felt like we had just moved to Florida—with the move into *our new house*. And I did not want to leave. I had not felt that anywhere in the last two years.

What an Abba Father! You have given your daughter just what she needed, a backyard of beautiful greenery—trees, bushes, plants, birds, and a backyard fence to boot. It was a retreat ground. A perfect place to spend time with the Creator.

Our one-and-a-third acre had a mini forest on the east side. One of the joys of the morning was to wake up, look out the eastern window, catch the colorful sunrise, sparkling leaves, and pine needles of the variegated greenery. I listened for each bird's chirp. The colors of the blue jay, red-headed woodpecker, and sometimes yellow finch stopped my parade. Sightings of the Florida Hawk and huge Sand Crane were spectacular and camera worthy.

I had two good days in my study preparing for the Moody

class and for the Toronto seminar. I rejoiced in the message God was giving me and I would be excited to share it. My life was starting to feel like it was "whole" –back together again. Like I was all here, and I wanted to be. *Thank you, Lord.* I had a major praise session.

I would not have traded these two dark years for anything, *but I would never choose them again or wish them on anyone else.*

"Lord, you have been good. You have given me health and strength. Even though I could not always find you, you were here. And in my desperation, you did shine through just when I could not go on. Thank you for those who ministered to me— loved me—even when I could not receive it. Thank you for that evidence of your presence."

"Thank you, Lord, most of all for loving me unconditionally and letting me feel that special love. Love that was not based on performance, rather just because *I am your daughter!* I still relish it and want to enjoy it forever."

Every time I read Jesus's words to Martha, I felt I was more like Mary. Yet, I did not think I was supposed to be sitting at Jesus feet listening. Rather women were to be in the kitchen preparing food, right? "Martha was distracted by all the preparations that had to be made. She came to him and asked, 'Lord, don't you care that my sister has left me to do the work by myself? Tell her to help me!" *Did Jesus?*

"Martha, Martha, the Lord answered, you are worried and

upset about many things, but few things are needed—or indeed only one. Mary has chosen what is better and it will not be taken away from her" (Luke 10:38-42).

Yes! Finally, confirmation of my greatest joy.

It was so refreshing—it was a love I had never known before.

I do not have to strive any more to prove anything. *I can just enjoy your love, Lord.* The overflow was so sweet and natural. I do not have to work at it just because I think "I should."

You even renewed my love for Jim. I see again what a wonderful person he is—what a beautiful human being. Thank you for restoring my sense of supporting him and caring for him—rather than just thinking of my own purposes.

The entire world looked different. I would say, "Thank you Lord for recharging my life."

—

Several months later, I faced a right breast biopsy. I already had a needle aspiration of a two-point-five-centimeter cyst in my left. On one hand I felt it was "routine," on the other I could not help but think about the possible outcome. *What if it was malignant?*

> Those of you who do not give up everything
> you have, cannot be my disciples. (Luke 14:33)

I knew you were asking me to give up my health— "Are you willing, Bev, to give your good health to me?

"Yes, Lord. It is all yours. Your will be done. I know you will be there with me and that is all I need."

November seventeen – the night before the surgery. How precious it was to play MBI's video "Perfect Peace." Thank you, Lord, for speaking directly to me and imparting your perfect peace that passes all understanding. These songs continued to touch my soul deeply, as they did at the Toronto Women's Ministry Seminar.

> As the deer pants for the water, so my soul longs after you.
>
> You alone are my heart's desire and I long to worship you.
>
> You alone are my strength, my shield.
>
> To you alone may my spirit yield
>
> You alone are my heart's desire and I long to worship you.[1]

—

> In moments like these, I sing out a song; I sing out a love song to Jesus
>
> In moments like these I lift my hands; I lift my hands to the Lord
>
> Singing I love you, Lord; singing, I love you, Lord.
>
> Singing, I love you, Lord: I love you.[2]

Lord, you are most important to me during this time. If your presence is with me, I will go through the valley of the shadow of death. It was no coincidence that I spoke on Psalm 23 the Tuesday before this surgery. I valued the beautiful picture of the shepherd's loving presence.

Thursday, November 18, 1993.

God provided excellent care for me at the hospital. Jim took Thursday and Friday off to be with me—what a sweetheart! I was so thankful for his care and willingness to accept whatever the Lord sent. Knowing the Lord would be with us, we were able to sleep the night before and had peace throughout the morning.

We had to wait until Monday, November 22 for results.

Tic toc, tic toc … And then …

Lord, my heart wanted to explode—results were benign!

I wanted to celebrate life. I made Jim's favorite meal. We ate by candlelight, with soft music. We celebrated life.

"Thank you, Lord for giving us more life together. You are so good. You have given us an unbelievable love for each other these twenty-five-plus years and now you have extended it. Thank you for leading me to stop and really take note. I am forty-six – my dad died when he was forty-nine. I wondered if you were going to call my life short on earth. I was ready to see you face to face—in fact, I was excited about that possibility. I longed to be with you—as a deer pants for water so my soul longs for you. The thought of being with you excited my soul deeply." It was a very emotional moment.

Yet the earthly ties would be hard to break. Obviously, the Lord had more for me to do. I am God's dearly loved. I am willing.

Thank you, Lord, for the opportunity to face death, that I might face life more fully!

More fully indeed.

The next two years held multiple state and national events—too many to list here. Many were speaking events at churches. Plus speaking at Pre-Evangelism Praying Conferences, Women in Evangelism Conference at the Billy Graham Center in Wheaton, and Decade of Promise in Chicago, and more. The Moody Bible Institute extension courses continued. Other events included developing teams for Florida Intercessory Network (FIN) and Ministry Wives International.

Women's Ministry at our church was greatly expanding. Multiple events and teams were formed. It was such a joy to serve with the woman at our church in Women's Bible Study, Prayer Shield, Real Treat, and Women of the Word study. My journal revealed continuing praise for God's Holy Spirit working through me and our team. Pages and pages of details surfaced praise, even all these years since. For example:

> Lord, I felt your presence especially powerful Saturday morning when I spoke about your unbelievable love to your daughters. *Every word*

flowed forth pristinely — that was clearly your Spirit! Women responded in powerful ways.

Another:

There is so much I could write about this event. I asked people to respond to God after the message. Many did. I was there until midnight. I wish I could write it all out. God's Spirit again was moving powerfully!

Revival and spiritual awakening were witnessed. Many in our network shared incredible stories of God's redeeming work. We held all night prayer vigils. God miraculously moved in obvious ways. The Holy Spirit visited us, in ways that were new to many attending. Yet, it was clear to each one, that this was God's Holy Spirit moving in a very personal and mighty way.

What a sovereign contrast to those first two years here in south Florida!

Thank you, precious Lord Jesus, for purifying and deepening the truth that I am God's dearly loved, *as is everyone on our team and network.*

Taken. Chosen. Broken.

… Truly home now – finally.

Chapter 28

Let it Go

Let it go. Let it go.

For now.

I tried. I could not.

I have a sense, Lord, that you are preparing me for something new. I feel you want me to continue giving away as many of my ministry roles as possible—for sure the administrative parts. I have had "feelings" of being in Portland--the smells, the sounds, the forests, the mountains...ahhh.

Jim returned from a Chicago meeting. We talked about the future. I could not believe what came out of my mouth. "I've been thinking about a new women's ministry course/program at Western Seminary and how someday I'd love to have *one* focus, teaching at a Bible college or seminary."

The next day Jim said I ought to update my resume and send it to Western Seminary.

Let it go.

The next morning, I woke up with Western Seminary on my mind and *again* I was overwhelmed with feelings of being in Portland. *Lord, I have said to you, please remove these feelings and these thoughts or fulfill them.*

I asked Jim what he meant. What *if* Western Seminary responded positively? Jim said, "We'd move to Portland."

I said, "Do you know what you are saying?"

He said, "Yes. I think you should just do it and see what they say."

"Are you serious?"

Let it go?

Lord, please do not give me the desires of my heart if they do not please you. *The last two mornings you have overwhelmed me with your love—your "lovingkindness," your "unfailing love" for me.* I am God's dearly loved.

Oh, Lord, tears are flowing. Something happened when Lorraine visited—she reflected it in her letter. She felt some healing had taken place. Lord, you gave her a visual of her future: grey clouds (where she is now), with cloudy mountains to climb to reach the sun filled sky (where she is headed). Is that a visual for us too? I have not felt I should pray about moving back to Portland, not in these four years we have been here.

Are these dates a coincidence?

August 20, today at 3:30 a.m. God told me clearly to resign FIN and MWNI.

August 20 is the date we left Orlando to move to Portland.

August 20 is the date we left Portland to move to south Florida

Lord, I do not know where this is going, but please hold my hand and lead me every step of the way. Do not let me go before or behind you.

"Truly my soul finds rest in God" (Ps 62:1).

God alone. *Lord may my soul rest in you and* you alone. *No matter where I am or where you are leading me to go.*

—

Jim told the church elders last night that he felt "burned out." He told them, "I don't know how long I can go on pastoring." He felt done.

I felt like the Lord was preparing us for a change. I felt the Lord was telling me to give up as much as I could of what he had given me here in South Florida, specifically Women's Ministry, FIN, and MBS. I felt like I needed to clear my slate.

I felt impressed, confirmed by Jim, to send my resume to Western Seminary in Portland. I started to, two weeks before the Leesburg retreat but felt overwhelmed—like I could not take the time then to put it together. So, I began to discount the whole idea.

And let it go.

It came back again. I read an ad in Christianity Today for Western Seminary. That prompted me to think about it *again*. Jim and I talked very openly about moving back to Portland, selling the house, and looking for employment in Portland.

Jim completed his Master of Pastoral Studies from Multnomah's Biblical Seminary on May 19, 1995. His last class was the day he turned fifty. It was a magnificent event to celebrate with family. We loved being there again for the commencement.

—

A week later, after returning home with Jim from a national conference, I felt I could not "let it go" another day. I went through the pain of trying to finish my resume *and* write a cover letter to Western Seminary. I did. I mailed it. I felt obedient.

And it was a relief to have it done.

It was so *unlikely* that would open a door. A resume in the mail from an unknown person—*a woman!* If it did, I would know it was God and God *alone*.

—

The next day we went on vacation at Toxaway, North Carolina with our dear friends, David and Carol. Precious time together in the beauty of God's creation, the cool mountains, the vegetation… I longed for more of God's beauty. God led me to the Psalms.

> When the LORD restored the fortunes of Zion, we were like those who dreamed. Our mouths were filled with laughter, our tongues with songs of Joy. Then it was said among the nations, 'The LORD has done great things for them.' The Lord has done great things for us, and we are filled with joy. Restore our fortunes, O LORD, like streams in the Negev. Those who sow in tears will reap with songs of joy. Those who go out weeping,

carrying seed to sow, will return with songs of joy
carrying sheaves with them. (Psalm 126)

... and may you live to see your children's
children." (Psalm 128:6a)

Lord, I believe you have clearly said this morning: Jerusalem
and Zion are Oregon (Portland), and Babylon is Florida, and
you are going to return us to Oregon to see our children's
children.

I was so grateful. I could not express my feelings. I simply
let tears flow.

God made it clear first in Jeremiah 29. That was the very
passage he spoke to me in 1992. I cried out, "Lord, will we have
to stay in Florida, or could we move back to Portland?"

God responded by saying: Jeremiah 29:28.

He has sent this message to us in Babylon: It
will be a long time. Therefore, build houses
(your word to us to build this house we are in
now) and settle down, plant gardens, and eat
what they produce.

I heard God say, "Settle down. This is where I want you for
now—maybe forever. Live as though it were."

Today God drew me back to this very same passage and led
me to those precious words of Jeremiah 29:10-14.

I will be found by you, declares the LORD, and
will bring you back from captivity....and will

bring you back to the place from which I carried you into exile.

This was confirmation that God was going to take us back to Oregon. We would be near our grandchildren and children. *Yes, Lord!*

Jim and I both had a desire not to be involved in church full-time, at least when we first moved back. We desired jobs in Christian colleges or organizations. We knew this did not pay much but were willing to live according to God's purpose for us. *Please, Lord, open a door for Jim—for employment, Lord. And for me in your time.*

I felt I should not take any speaking commitments beyond January 1996; that I should keep my calendar clear. All I had were two more MBI classes---tomorrow and the next Saturday.

Was it possible we would be gone by then? Given our past, it certainly was.

Remember how quickly the Lord moved us from Orlando to Portland. God sold our house in twenty-four hours. Moving from Portland to Palm Beach Gardens--this move—God sold our home in forty-eight hours. Nothing is impossible with God!

Please make it clear to Jim and me where and when you want us to move. Please sell our house quickly to confirm it.

Lord, I thank you that I can rest in you—and I do.

I let it go ... *directly to you, Lord!*

Chapter 29

Jitterbug

Gramma Connie? My mom? Doing the jitterbug?

Wait. Cannot be.

We were taught you could not dance. It was not allowed.

And here was my mom dancing like she had done it all her life.

Not when I lived at home, she didn't.

Dan and Mo, Lorraine and Gene, Jim and me, plus our Portland friends Dick and Jeree Clark--we all witnessed it.

We were in disbelief.

Then we began laughing with joy. Loved it! Who would have guessed? It was a gift watching Mom enjoy herself so much that she broke out in a jitterbug. Never thought I would see that. What a fun time. A great celebration!

Dana Point, California. We were celebrating Dan and Maureen's marriage. A timely trip west while processing our immediate future.

We could not be happier with the wife our son chose, and their walk with God. We were so grateful. We so enjoyed the reception, the food, the people and yes, the jitterbug.

Who could not enjoy this family celebration? It was one of our best.

It was a peaceful feeling to see our two children marry great spouses. Spouses who know the Lord and respect their mates. It is one of the greatest gifts in life to feel close to them. And to feel that fully reciprocated.

—

Jim and I went from the wedding to the Los Angeles Fasting and Prayer '95 Conference. We agreed to go because dear people thought we should, and they provided the money. It gave us another Sunday "off" and a few days in between. Both were good for someone in "burnout."

We stayed for a few sessions, then left. We needed more processing, more prayer.

And then we ate.

Hearing Joe Aldrich again and then Vonette Bright stirred my heart. Memories flooded in of our previous days in Portland. We both wanted more.

Four days later we arrived back home in Florida. That evening the church elders came to our home to hear Jim's decision to move back to Portland.

I could not believe my eyes, or my ears. They initially could not respond, could not pray. They cried—each one of them. They told Jim what he meant to them. Jim wept with them.

Days earlier Jim met with a well-respected national leader. After a few sentences from Jim to explain what he was feeling, Kevin Dyer's answer was clear, concise, and conclusive.

1. You have ministry burn-out.
2. You need to take a year off ministry.
3. You need to go home—return to Portland, where your kids are.
4. You need to do it soon—do not drag it out. Six months is too long. Do it within three or four months.
5. Take the next step and God will meet you. Do not sit around waiting.

That was clear confirmation. Both of us cried after we realized the things we had been feeling and thinking were legitimate.

God was moving us back "home."

Jitterbug anyone?

—

The second couple who looked at our house came back the next day and made an offer that night. Jim woke up the next morning thinking we should accept the offer if no others were made before ten a.m.

None were made.

Jim did not even counteroffer. Ron, who appraised it, thought it was a great offer. So that confirmed it. We signed a contract at five p.m.

—

The next day Jim got a call from Eagle Fern Camp in Estacada, Oregon. They asked if he was interested in filling a position at camp, either Program Director or Facilities Manager.

Facilities Manager seemed perfect because it would not involve a whole lot of "new" learning. Right now, Jim needed something he could easily slide into without a lot of pressure. Also, Jim would not be responsible for the whole camp. The Camp Director would be.

That should relieve some pressure. The Camp Director wanted the Facilities Manager position filled as soon as possible. That position had just become available. It had not even been publicized yet.

Jim got the Facilities Manager job.

—

Becoming God's dearly loved means letting the truth of our *being dearly loved* become enfleshed in everything we think, say, and do.

My mom said she prayed all night for us last night.

Jitterbug anyone?

Being God's Dearly Loved

Being God's dearly loved means letting the truth of our *being dearly loved* become enfleshed in everything we think, say, or do. It typically comes in four phases.

1. Taken 2. Chosen. 3. Broken. **4. Given**

—

4. GIVEN

"I will strengthen you and help you.

I will uphold you with my righteous right hand." (Isaiah 41:10)

We are taken, chosen, and broken, to be given.

Why has it taken me a lifetime *to live as God's dearly loved*?

Our greatest fulfillment in being *God's dearly loved* comes in giving ourselves to others. Our gifts are the many ways in which we express who we are as

God's dearly loved.

Who can we be for God and each other?

I am still learning and wondering, what do I have to give?

... and you?

Chapter 30

You Didn't Bring Us This Far

He didn't bring us this far to leave us
He didn't teach us to swim to let us drown
He didn't build his home in us to move away
He didn't lift us up to let us down. 1

I remembered sitting in my car in our driveway in Orlando, Florida, ready to begin my first ever drive to Oregon. Leaving everything familiar, I visualized a covered wagon heading west. This song by the Imperials came on the radio. Tears flooded my eyes.

Once again, we were moving to Oregon. Yes!

This time from Palm Beach Gardens, Florida.

"He didn't teach us to swim to let us drown."
Really?

Oregon was declared a disaster area. The Willamette River was predicted to overflow into downtown Portland. "Willamette Valley Flood of 1996."

Yes. We were arriving during "the Great Flood of '96."

How would we ever find a place to live in the middle of a disaster? A flood.

We put our stuff in a storage unit. We drove around in the pouring rain, looking at apartments and modular homes.

"He didn't teach us to swim to let us drown."
Uh...huh.

It seemed impossible to get a place with our new budget, to rent or buy. That was a hard adjustment. There were many lovely places to live but only within our previous budget.

I felt pressure to bring in a second income. I wondered if I should begin job searching. I did not feel up to it. But if I could supplement our income perhaps things would look different.

"He didn't bring us this far *to leave us.*"

Holly Ridge Apartments were near Lorraine and Gene's home in Gresham. We liked it. They had no three-bedroom available. They did not know when they would.

"...to leave us?"

Jim stopped by on Sunday and asked if there was one available. They said no. He was disappointed. He felt sure God wanted us there.

Lorraine called again on Monday. *They had one.* We could not see it until Wednesday, but we could put a deposit on it. We did. Later we learned it *was available* on the Sunday Jim stopped by, but the person he talked to did not know it.

"He didn't bring us this far *to leave us.*" True!

Jim started his job at Camp Eagle Fern the first weekend we arrived. He would be gone three weekends in a row. This Saturday was the only one in three weeks Jim would be available to move. "If this apartment is for us, please, Lord, confirm that tonight and enable us to move on Saturday." God did!

"He didn't build his home in us *to move away.*"

The key was available to us only before five p.m. on Friday. We made it. Everything was clean. I was so thankful for our new home and for our dear friends who helped us move—yes, everything up three flights of stairs, including my piano.

Saturday, the move was complete. Saturday night Jim spent his first night at camp. I spent my first night alone in our new apartment.

The next morning, I journaled an extensive list to *thank you, Lord,* which included:

- A good night's sleep. Your protection in this new quiet place to live.
- Genuine peace and faith in Jesus.
- A great Sunday at church with Lorraine and Gene. Tears of joy. I felt your Spirit.

  "My help comes from the LORD, the Maker of heaven and earth. He will not let your foot slip ... The LORD watches over you ... the LORD will watch over your coming and going both now and forevermore. (Psalm 121: 2, 3a, 5a, 8)

Lord, thank you for showing me the first morning: God takes the initiative when he wants you to join him in his work, per Henry Blackaby, *Experiencing God.* 3

- God called Noah
- God called Abraham
- God called Moses

My role was to focus on my love relationship with the Lord. Only he could open my spiritual eyes to see where he was at work around me and invite me to join him.

We are taken, chosen, and broken, *to be given.*

Given.

To whom, what, where Lord?

Thank you, Lord for this anxiety reliever. Thank you for peace that I can trust you to take the initiative in showing me what you want me to do.

You Lord *have* brought us this far

... To be given.

Chapter 31

Startled

I was *startled.*

My dad was "sweating great drops of blood." He was sitting on the ground in his garden. He was not working. He was simply there. Mom and us kids stood around watching him. We did nothing to help him. We thought he needed air and space. I started crying. Deep convulsive sobs. Everyone else just stood there emotionless. After a while, he curled up in a shrunken state.

I knew he was "gone." My sobs intensified.

And then I awoke.

It was 25 years ago—June 1st, 1971—that my dad died.

I had never sobbed like I did in that dream. I never really grieved his absence since I was in Germany when he died and was not able to fly home in time for the funeral. It was hard to face the reality of his death.

Dad never saw his first granddaughter—Lorraine—before he died. Mom said he loved showing pictures of her. His first grandson—Dan---was born six months after Dad's death.

For a couple of years after his death, I dreamed multiple times that he walked into my room. I responded in surprise and joy believing he was alive. Every time.

Startled. Again.

I found the poem Dad wrote to me on my 15the birthday. Mom decoupaged it for me.

The last stanza read:

> …. For the future then as you look ahead,
> Woman of wisdom may it ever be said
> Spirit-filled and led, may you always be seen
> As sweet as when you were just fifteen.

Tears fell onto the plaque. *Oh, how I want to be, Lord!*

> I talked about his death several times that year.
> I was forty-nine.
> Dad was forty-nine when he died.
> That was all he got.

Maybe that is why he filled every moment he had with serving or telling someone about Jesus—even migrant workers living outside-of-town in scary slum areas.

Dad loved his family. He cared about people.

For the last six months I wondered if God would give me longer than my dad.

It was a mixed blessing. There were so many things yet to experience—the joys of having grandchildren, watching your own children parent and grow in the Lord, new friends to enjoy, new opportunities for ministry and service.

And yet, Lord, to be with you is far better. To see your face, to join the angels and others gone before me already in your presence, worshipping, praising, and adoring you, Lord Jesus. How I long to experience you without the interference of sin, evil, and the world. What ecstasy it must be. To praise you, Lord, without limitation or hindrances, without inhibitions— freely and fully!

Dad is.

And has for 25 years.

—

Several months ago, we left south Florida and moved back to Oregon.

I heard the Spirit of God telling me to call Western Seminary and ask if I could teach one course. There had been no response to my resume sent from south Florida months ago.

More than *startled*.

God, isn't that a male dominated, academic institution? *I am neither. That is scary.*

Remember the job hunts years ago? Nothing at Western Seminary. I tried.

Okay God. If this is of you, I will wait for you to tell me the exact day, time, and words.

Tuesday morning, I was sitting quietly praying. I felt the Spirit of God prompt me. "Call Western Seminary today and ask for an appointment with the Faculty Dean, Dr. Jim Sweeney."

Marilyn answered. She said the person I needed to talk to was not in. However, Marilyn would have Bonnie call me.

Sure.

Been here. Done that.

Meantime, several other job offers were brought to my attention by friends. Vision House. Luis Palau. Pilgrims. MBC. NW Medical Teams. *Where should I apply?*

—

It was 3:30 a.m. I could not sleep. *What is it, Lord? Do you have something to tell me? I want to hear your voice. I need direction.*

That morning Jim was packing to stay three days and two nights at Eagle Fern Camp, *again.* He was working as Facilities Manager. The camp was filled throughout the year with retreats and conferences, most on weekends. He was constantly needed there.

Again, I was alone. I felt sad.

Jim had only taken one day off since camp season started. We had an enjoyable day together. But when he returned, he decided he could not be gone from camp on a Saturday again. On this day, I would have liked to be with Jim. I would have liked to have a day off together. I missed him.

When he came home at night he would sit on the couch, turn TV on and fall asleep. He slept all evening. He woke up at four or five a.m., got up and went back to work. I kept waiting for things to change, for him to get caught up on sleep or camp work. But the reality was beginning to sink in.

It was not going to happen.

Startling.

The voice in my head again said, *I want you to meet my expectations.* I tried to lower my expectations so I would not be disappointed. I was tired of being disappointed. Apparently, my expectations still were not low enough.

Would I ever have joy or fun again? *Is that voice telling me a lie or the truth?*

Maybe I was really missing my friends from Florida. It was hard to finally have a free day (moving was completed) and have no one to share it with. Oh, there were women with whom I could have met. But frankly, of all the possibilities I really would have liked to relax with my husband. I did not want to be feeling sorry for myself. I just felt a need to express my feelings somehow. Eventually I assumed it would need to be to my journal. Not the same.

It seemed when I expressed thoughts of Jim taking time off, he took it as a challenge not to. That is how it felt. So, I said little about it. But that did not work either.

I did not understand.

Sometimes I felt I could not wait and hope any longer. I needed to accept the fact that Jim would always work like this. I needed to plan my life accordingly, to fill it with other people and activities. But these were only substitutes. They did not fill the need to enjoy my husband.

Is that an unrealistic expectation, Lord?

In biblical times, did husbands and wives enjoy each other socially and emotionally? Or did they just spend their day providing and surviving? Was the union based on supplying a home to raise a family? He worked outside. She worked inside.

Last time I felt an ache of loneliness, Lord, you seemed to fill it. Is that what this is about? Do I need to draw closer to you, to spend more time with you, Lord? Please show me.

I felt like I wanted someone to care for me. Lorraine probably felt the same way after working hard for a week. Jim may have wanted the same thing. I did not know. There may be three people here needing to be cared for and no one to care for them. It seemed the mom and wife should be the caring, nurturing person here. Right? Perhaps I needed to get off my duff and begin caring for them. And in that find joy and fulfillment.

Off I went, to Lorraine's, to help her clean the house. She said she was under a huge time crunch, with work and her husband's activities. She was so grateful. I really enjoyed helping someone else. Good choice. And it took my mind off myself.

Just as I got home, so did Jim.

We talked. I cried. We both had hard days.

"I don't like being with people," he said.

"But ... I am a people." I responded.

Silence.

Lord, now what?

It was true that Jim's heavy involvement in whatever job he had was a motivator for me also to bury myself in my job or ministry because there is nothing to come home to—he was gone or busy. It was especially hard because I had not connected with people, and I felt at least I could at work. I was willing to take it slow waiting for a job, but now I felt I needed to pursue something. I needed a life too.

The voice in my head speaking lies was finally silenced by the truth.

➢ Jesus through his Holy Spirit will speak to your expectations.
➢ Jesus through his Holy Spirit brings real, full joy.

Peace was beginning to replace *being startled* ....

———

The next morning Jim and I got up late and went out for brunch. We went to camp together, from there to Clackamas Mall, then home. It was an enjoyable day together.

I did not realize the impact "burnout" had on a person. Yes, Jim left his last job in a state of "burnout." He pastored broken people. I did not realize at the time that *we are all broken.* He liked the maintenance job because he was not involved with people's problems. He was exceptionally good at fixing *things*.

Jim soon realized he needed help. He was not himself. He was not who he wanted to be. He was simply trying to cope. At camp, he could be alone in the maintenance shop or work on the campgrounds. He was not involved in the people part of camp.

He knew it was time. He made appointments with a reputable counselor. He went.

I went to the internet. *Psychology Today* defined burnout as a "state of emotional, mental, and often physical exhaustion brought on by prolonged or repeated stress. Though it is most often caused by problems at work, it can also appear in other areas of life." 1

Jim recognized exhaustion, irritability, and withdrawal as daily feelings. He admitted, "I would rather be alone. I dread going to work with people."

Jim realized he started work at camp after having an extensive list of responsibilities in Florida that led to, "I can't do this anymore." The list involved pressure and pain on every level, nearly all out of his control. Jim realized he had had these symptoms for some time, and they seemed to be increasing in intensity. He was ready to begin the needed work toward health.

Healing began. It took time. Medicine helped. Counseling was essential.

Today Jim would say the support system he began building into his life "shored me up during those times." Extensive exploration of the truths he embraced, generated life-giving health and joy. They made a lasting impact. He began sharing, teaching, and building them into his life. He would summarize it using an invaluable resource, *The Ascent of a Leader,* by Bill Thrall, Bruce McNicol, and Ken McElrath.

Transparency is letting you see the cracks in my life, but vulnerability is letting people *I trust* fill those cracks. 2

His discoveries were life changing. For him. For me. For us.

And beyond.

Dearly loved. Given.

Chapter 32

I Have Something to Tell You

"I have something to tell you."

I was sitting in our small breakfast nook looking out the window at the beautiful roses in our garden: Double Delight, Queen Elizabeth, Abraham Lincoln – six varieties in all. Each chosen and planted to celebrate the birth of each of our grandchildren. The sky was blue, the sun warming, and I was enjoying my morning mocha. My husband brought over his cherry mocha and sat beside me. We smiled, wondering how we would spend this first vacation day.

My nearly eighty-year-old mother, Connie, flew all the way from Florida to visit us in our new house in Oregon. Each time she came we wondered if it would be her last. We loved our time together—lots of laughs and good memories. Lots of sweet pictures. She seemed to be in relatively good health, considering her age, and we looked forward to spending this first day seeing some of nature's beauty in the Northwest. She always enjoyed it too.

Mom walked up to our table. We offered her a seat and asked if she wanted some hot chocolate to drink. Mom never drank coffee or tea.

She remained standing. No response. Facial lines tightened. Her eyes focused on the floor. Silence. Deep breath. Suddenly she blurted out, fast and forceful, "I have something to tell you.

When I was a teenager, I was raped. I had a baby girl. I gave her up for adoption."

She stopped. Looked down. She took a breath, relieved. Silence.

Shock would not be a strong enough word to describe our feelings.

Silence. Ummm…. More silence. *What did she just say? Did I hear her correctly?*

I eventually was able to say, "Mom, what happened? Where is she? Can we find her?"

"No. I don't want you to find her. Every day I pray for her—that she would be loved and blessed by the parents who adopted her. It was a closed adoption. I don't want her to know how she was conceived. I want her to grow up feeling loved and wanted."

Whew… "What happened, Mom?"

Mom wouldn't say much about the father or the specifics. It was clearly unwanted and forced. She said when she discovered she was pregnant and told her parents, her mother was enraged.

"She raised her arms to hit me. She ordered me, 'Get out of this house immediately and don't come back until you have gotten rid of *that thing*!' I was scared for my life."

"Where did you go, Mom?"

"Well, I learned that the Salvation Army Residential Facility in Chicago would house pregnant teens until the birth and then help them make arrangement for adoption. I took the bus and lived there until the baby was born."

Mom didn't talk a lot about the pain of each day—knowing how this baby came to be---the shock, the force, the unexpected invasion, violation. There was no reprisal, no retaliation for the rape.

My mom told me that the peaceful, forgiving, accommodating environment of the Residential Facility contrasted each painful emotion. Give her baby up for adoption? Yet believing this precious baby could have a better life somewhere else brought momentary comfort. And hope.

What if she brought this baby back home? Where does a teen girl go to provide all that is needed for a baby? She had not even finished high school. There was no place. Rent? A job? Impossible. Certainly not at her parent's home. Her parents would not allow it. Her only hope was that a kind couple would adopt the baby and she would have a good life—one a single teenaged mom could not provide. So, her thoughts rested in that hope. Most days.

"I had no choice but to go back home after the baby was given up for adoption. It was hard. When I arrived back home, my parents and siblings all acted like nothing ever happened and I was not allowed to talk about it. I assumed the disgrace was too great. I felt deep shame."

I asked if my siblings, Carole, Paul, or Palmer knew.

"Yes, I told them right before I came to visit you. I wanted to tell you in person."

"Mom, are you sure you don't want us to find her?"

"No. Clearly no. Let her enjoy her life with her adoptive parents. I don't want to ruin it for her. I just thought you should know."

Okay, hot chocolate. "Here, Mom." I reached to refill my cup with more coffee.

Mom did not want to talk any more about her painful memories. It was hard to honor her desire. But we did, for the rest of her visit with us.

I of course was eager to talk with my sister about it. Carole *really* wanted to look for this sister we did not know we had. We did not even know how to find her since it was a closed adoption.

I thought we should respect Mom's wishes, since Mom choose to tell us. Carole reluctantly agreed. For now.

Mom could have kept it a secret forever, I think…

Chapter 33

God, If You Are There

Sometime later, Mom revealed more of her story.

After my mom, Connie, returned home to Indiana from the Salvation Army Residential Facility in Chicago, she knelt beside her bed and said, "God if you are there, I want to be a good girl and marry a good man."

That was all she knew to say as a teenager feeling so alone. She was not even sure God existed. At that point, she just knew she wanted a different life than the one she saw her family living.

Connie was the youngest of her four siblings. Her family thrived on alcohol. Her parents drank consistently. They argued constantly. When Connie's mom said it was too hot, her dad said it was not. When her dad said it was time for dinner, her mom said it was not. Connie did not remember her parents ever agreeing—on anything. They certainly had no kind words for Connie—the child they did not want or need. They already had too many mouths to feed.

Connie's dad worked as hard as he could, as his dad before him since immigrating. Life seemed to only set you up to die, he said. No one seemed to know how to avoid the physical labor that accompanied emotional desperation. She felt she only added to her parents' hard life. She did not know how to change that. She tried to go unnoticed and simply hide.

As the youngest child watching an all-too-real-life-movie of her family, she was determined not to follow their path. She said she never took a drink of alcohol. And was determined, never would. Eventually, her two brothers died from cirrhosis of the liver.

If anyone mentioned God or religion, her parents simply responded by saying they were Catholic—they lived in a heavily populated Catholic part of the country—although they never, ever went to church or knew anything about it. They simply said, "Don't talk to us about God. We are Catholic." End of conversation.

There was constant yelling, pain, cursing, riotous evenings … No, Connie wanted to start a different path than the one she had lived. She wanted to start a new chapter.

—

The next week Connie noticed a church down the street. She wanted to go, but was not sure they would let her in. Filled with shame and turmoil, she hesitated. Yet, it seemed her only hope. She decided to try and walk in. What could they do? Simply tell her to leave, right? It was worth a try.

They let her in! It was fall and they were planning a Christmas play. They asked for volunteers. Connie got up her courage and asked if they would let her participate. They said, "Yes!"

Connie cried.

She felt so unworthy. Yet they accepted her.

The genuine acceptance she felt at that moment touched a painfully empty space that had never been filled. The tenderness of someone touching that spot for the first time in her life would bring tears well into adulthood. That was a first.

As a young teen she longed for more. She wondered, is it possible to feel loved in this life beyond this moment? Genuinely loved? Not for what someone can get from you. But simply loved *as you are?*

After church Connie returned home only to have her parents tell her if she wanted to live there, she must quit high school and go earn some money to support the household—to put food and drinks on the table. She so wanted to finish high school, but realized she had no other option. So, she did what they were demanding.

Connie got a job at Bendix Corporation in South Bend.

One day she had a conversation with a co-worker that led to the question, "Are you religious, Connie? Because if you are, there is a man over there who is religious too. I think you should meet him." She introduced Connie to co-worker, Raymond White.

Ray was a genuine follower of Jesus. Connie soon learned that Ray read the Bible and prayed daily. He loved talking to her about the Lord Jesus. She loved hearing!

It was all new to Connie, something for which she had a deep longing.

She began to realize, *God is here!*

"You mean I can have a genuine relationship with him? *How?*"

"Yes, Connie. And he loves you "just as you are!" Ray would say.

"*Me?* How can that be?" She wondered.

Over the next days, further reading and conversations together eventually lead her to believe the words she read in the Bible. Connie believed Jesus Christ's death on the cross for the forgiveness of sins, included hers. And she clearly received God's forgiveness. Her longing for truth and a deeper understanding simply grew. Peace in her spirit was a new experience. She felt God's love in a way she never had.

Someone genuinely loved her *as she is?* And that "someone" was really God and his son Jesus? Why had she never heard this before in her whole life?

Later in life she would say Ray "discipled me."

—

Three years later Ray White asked Connie Edwards to marry him, and she was delighted to say, "yes!" They were married on August 1, 1945, in South Bend, Indiana.

Those first months of life together were beautiful in multiple ways. They bought a house in the suburbs, with a lovely yard, met neighbors, and began attending a local church together. It felt like a new life.

And it was.

Their first child was brought into the world with immense joy on December 10, 1946. Connie felt like she was on a new planet. And, well, she was. This baby would be loved by her mother *and* father—and whoever else met her. This baby was wanted. It could be known by *everyone* that this baby was conceived *by them* and would be raised *by them*. God would provide all that was needed to bring this daughter to know him early in her life. What a joy.

Ray made a wooden cradle in which to lay her. They thought she might be musical like Connie or like one of their favorite vocalists, George Beverly Shea, on the Billy Graham team. The perfect name for her: Beverly Lae, rhymes with Beverly Shea.

She slept well. She had dark hair and dark eyes, like Connie. She seemed content and was a blessing to hold. Each day was a joy for Connie, although admittedly there were moments when the past would resurface.

Time seemed to pass quickly as Beverly was healthy and easy to care for. Nearly one year later, Beverly contracted bronchitis. It was serious. The medical doctor said he had done all he could. He told Ray and Connie to take Beverly home and *keep on a steam-filled tent over her.* It was the *only* chance she would survive.

But hour after hour Beverly seemed to get worse.

Who could sleep? Who could eat? Neither Ray nor Connie wanted anything else but to remain by this baby's side. "God, you wouldn't take this one from us, would you? She was conceived in love and has been a daily blessing to us." Connie was especially broken at the possibility. "God, surely you will give her life. *Please God!"*

Ray prayed again and again...finally out loud. He then turned to Connie and said, "I believe God is telling us that Beverly will live; that God has a special plan for her life. I believe God is telling us *to take off the steam-filled tent over her."*

Ray did.

And Beverly began to breathe on her own. God gave her *life.*

---God *is* surely here, Connie!

Chapter 34

She Would Say

I wish when Mom was still with us, I was mature enough to understand. Or to ask insightful questions. She experienced challenge after challenge. Yet, each time she got back up and kept going.

Mom would say, "God gives me the strength. *Only God.*"

Clearly, God did.

After losing the love of her life, Ray, to a heart value malfunction, she began taking steps to get back up. She was only forty-seven years old. She always wanted to finish high school. She began taking courses. After a GED she went into Office Administration. Later, training as a Nurse Practitioner. Then got an Associate Degree in Cosmetology. Each one led to an excellent job and satisfying experiences.

She still missed Ray.

A valued friend at church said he knew someone she should meet.

Walter was in town from Virginia Beach, Virginia. His wife died of cancer four years previous. Mom took each step slow, but eventually felt living with a Jesus follower might enhance her life.

Walter came a second time to visit, and this time stayed with us in our house in Florida. He was a good man. It seemed a bit strange that he could not find the bathroom, although it was the room next to his bedroom. Each day, Walter needed a map to get to mom's house, five minutes away.

They married.

Then he made it clear, they had to live in his house in Virginia, not Mom's house in Florida.

That was unexpected.

The landline phone calls from mom made me wonder.

Mom wanted to get a new little kitchen window valence.

Walter's response was startling. "No. That one lasted twenty-five years. It will last twenty-five more. We do not need a new one."

Mom asked. "Bev, do you think I moved to the right place? I am beginning to wonder."

She was hopeful church would provide friends and comfort. She got to play the organ. She loved it!

Until she was accused of being too active, too visible. Women should be silent in the church.

My visit to their house opened my eyes to a unique relationship. Mom went to bed early, as usual. Walter stayed up until midnight or later. I slept in the guestroom. I woke up about eleven p.m. and heard Walter's voice. He was praying aloud for his two sons and their families. Then he began praying for mom and us--her four married children. He prayed like he knew God intimately.

He did.

His love for Jesus oozed out in those quiet moments. He would never miss church. It was his local family. All twenty-five people.

Eventually Mom began to see that he was having difficulty keeping the days straight.

"Tonight is church."

"No, Walter. This is Tuesday. Church is Wednesday."

"No. Tonight is church."

Mom thought it best to drive to church and he could see. They did.

"I don't understand why no one came to church tonight! That is sad!"

His diminishing memory soon led Mom to more urgent steps. She called his two adult sons. They disbelieved her and said when he talked on the phone, he was fine.

Mom grew more concerned. For his safety. For her safety.

Eventually Walter needed a minor medical procedure. She arranged with the doctor to give him a dementia test while in the office. She knew he would never agree to go just for *that*.

Sure enough.

His sons still did not believe Mom. Until she planned for *them* to meet with the doctor.

Finally.

Now what?

How would she navigate this chapter? She knew she could not do it alone.

She amazed me! Can you imagine all the pieces of the puzzle that had to fit together to make this plan work?

"Only God," Mom would say.

She put Walter's house up for sale. She packed. She asked my brothers to come up to Virginia Beach to drive a rental truck back to her house in central Florida. There she had arranged for Walter to be admitted into a Senior Health Care Facility in Orlando. At the same time, she moved back into her house.

She was moving back home.

She was welcomed home by my siblings and her church family. What a blessing!

Daily she visited Walter. She cared lovingly for him. Until he went to heaven.

Then she was on her own. This time she opened a beauty salon in her own home.

The story does not end there.

I wish it did.

I have more to tell you.

—

A few years later, my sister helped my mom buy a duplex nearer my sister's home in Oviedo, Florida. It was a good move for both. She loved it. Mom found a new church family. She did some volunteer work while there. Mom made healthy choices on every level. Food. Exercise. Family. Church. Neighbors.

Mom loved playing her organ, mandolin, banjo. She sang when she was younger. She loved music, especially hymns now.

She walked around the neighborhood twice a day. She loved exercising. She was in good shape. She drove herself to the nearby grocery store, and church.

Sometime later we began to wonder about her safety. How many times can you run a stop sign and miss getting hit? A traffic light?

Mom called. "I do not understand why it's dark outside. It is only ten o'clock. I wanted to walk today."

It was ten p.m.

"Mom, how did you get those cuts on your foot?"

"I don't know."

"Doesn't it hurt? They are bleeding."

"No."

"Could it be the broken glass on the floor?"

My sister's concern grew. The risk of Mom hurting herself increased at night. She did not know what time it was. She did not see dangers inside or out.

And then I got the call from my sister, *"Bev, I think it is time to put mom into a care center.* There is an incredibly good

Memory Care Center right here in Oviedo. It would be close by. *Will you come and tell her?"*

———

I sat down on the floor beside Mom. She stared at the stack of pictures.

I asked Mom, "Who is that?" A picture of her and my dad.

"I don't know." Mom recognized neither.

How do you tell your mom that it would be better for her to move into a Memory Care facility? Once the words came out, she cried. *"Not now. Please!"*

Did she really understand what I was saying? Sometimes she seemed to. Other times, no.

After more tears and conversation, we agreed *not* to move her then. Mom needed more care. We hired a dear woman to come in during the day. She could make sure mom got food. And was safe.

With her help, my mom started going through her stuff. My sister helped decide what went to which sibling. Mom could take only essentials into the care center.

Months went by. Mom still loved walking in her neighborhood. Her caregiver did not go with her. She was not as physically fit as Mom. Mom walked but could not find her way home. Fortunately, neighbors knew and sent her home, multiple times. Then they told my sister.

I flew down and toured the care center. They had a program

to stimulate residents. Each day was planned and carried out with supervision. There was room for mom.

How does someone who is used to living on her own, her own bedrooms, kitchen, living room, bathrooms, garage, and yard, adjust to sharing *every* room, including a bedroom, with a stranger? There was no outside walking. A small yard with chairs. Kind caretakers.

Will Mom know the difference?

Alzheimer's disease is brutal. Why don't they have a cure?

Mom went through so many challenges in life. She picked herself up and moved on. Each time. *Only God* she would say.

This time?

She deserved a Nobel Prize. Grammy Award. Lifetime Achievement Award.

Not Alzheimer's disease.

Not Memory Care Center.

A gold crown in heaven...

—

Nearly twenty years after Mom's *I have something to tell you* at our breakfast table in Oregon, our daughter Lorraine got an email. She was not sure if it was legit. Someone named Kym asked about Lorraine's family. She found us on Ancestory.com and was curious. Who wanted to know? Scam? Or?

Lorraine's name came up, along with mine on her search.

Kym's mother, Barbara had been given up for a closed adoption at the Salvation Army Residential Facility in Chicago, Illinois.

The door began to open.

In memory I heard my mom say, *"I have something to tell you"*

Mom went to be with her precious Lord Jesus two years earlier.

She might be looking down from heaven and rejoicing in her years of prayers for that precious "unknown" daughter.

She had reason to be!

I am sure she prayed every day of her life for Barbara.

—

Barbara and her husband Bob spend winters in St. Augustine Florida, summers in Michigan. My sister, Carole, who lives in Florida got to meet her first. FaceTime included me. Months later we took an RV trip to meet her. What a blessing!

All three of us sisters were amazed at similarities in skills, gifts, and joys in life.

Music, teaching, art, gardening, and Jesus.

"Teaching about the Christian way of life was my vocation, along with providing the best possible educational opportunities for children." Barbara's own words.

That summed up Barbara's extensive resume. She taught piano on the college level and home studio. She played the organ in churches, was a choir director. She was Principal at several Catholic schools in Michigan, thirty-two years.

Barbara and Bob have four children and eight grandchildren.

Barb was raised as an only child by loving adoptive parents.

Mom's prayers were heard ... and answered.

As Mom would say, *only God.*

Chapter 35

Farmer's Daughter

My destiny?

A farmer's daughter in Knox, Indiana. That is how my life started.

I love farms. At six-years-old it was fun.

Until a medical doctor told us that our only hope for my brother's health was to move to a warmer climate. We did. We acquired ten acres in the country near Apopka, Florida, across from orange groves. A small gardening plot was my at-home fun, grades one through twelve.

—

The "farmer" in me remains. The location simply changes, inside and outside plants.

What farmer's daughter would *even think* about teaching in a seminary?

What is a seminary?

Fast forward.

"Hello."

"I am Bonnie from Western Seminary. Remember me? Seven years ago, you were on campus, and I was the one who talked with you. I was Human Resource Director then. I always thought you should be part of the Western family. Now I work for the faculty.

I was so excited when Marilyn told me you called and wanted to meet with the Dean of Faculty, Dr. Sweeney. Dr. Sweeney will be so glad to meet you. I made an appointment for you on Thursday, 10:30 to 12:00. Do you think that will be enough time? Dr. sweeney will want lots of time to talk with you, I'm sure, Bev. Please know I am in your court and rooting for you!"

What? Who? Me?

A farmer's daughter?

—

Thursday finally came.

I simply shared with Dr. Sweeney a bit of my heart for ministry to women. I briefly shared my ministry experiences with women on east coast, west coast and overseas. It seemed only a few minutes before he spread his arms out as far as they would go. "I think you can do whatever you want here."

What? Really? What does that mean? Is the door *really that open?*

Dr. Sweeney said the president needed to meet me, so we walked into the middle of a meeting, and he introduced me. *In the middle of the meeting, the president greeted me.*

As we left, Dr. Sweeney told me Western Seminary (WS) wanted to develop a program for women—pastor's wives and women preparing for ministry. But WS was not sure how. "We are open to new ideas." Dr. Sweeney said he would call me Monday after Spring Break to talk about the next step.

Should I hold my breath? *Would he call me? Really?* Seemed unlikely...

The president called the next day to set up an appointment to meet on Tuesday. *Oh Lord, help! I cannot believe this is happening.* Well, it is not really, not yet.

Henry Blackaby's *Experiencing God* study again brought comfort. Is that why God had me go through it multiple times in south Florida? He knew I would need it. *I do! Now.*

While you are waiting on God:

1. You will be watching circumstances, asking God for his perspective.
2. You will be praying for a passion to know God, his purposes, and his ways.
3. You will be continually active in seeking, asking, and knocking.
4. You continue doing the last thing God told you to do.

> "In waiting you are shifting the responsibility of the outcome to God—where it belongs. He will accomplish through you more in days and weeks than you could ever accomplish in years of labor. Waiting on Him is always worth the wait. His timing and His ways are always right."[1]

Thank you, Lord for the comfort this has been to me while I have been in the waiting room. Thank you for proving yourself true, trustworthy. If the door at Western Seminary opens, it will clearly be God, only God.

Is an appointment with the president really going to happen on Tuesday?

Lord, please give me health, strength, vision, direction, and confidence in you. Thank you for helping me to feel stronger this afternoon—after stomach/intestinal flu or unhealthy food. What a night of stomach pain and aches.

—

All yesterday afternoon, evening, and night I had the same gastro pain—from that restaurant lunch. I finally got rid of it this morning. I prayed it would be gone before I met with Dr. Hawkins. I ate nothing. Drank water. Finally took a donnatal tablet thirty minutes before my appointment.

I went in feeling weak and dull.

On the drive home, I could not remember much of what was said. I barely made it home before falling asleep. Medication had never done that to me before. I slept sound, all night.

The next day I felt terrible about the interview. I blew it. After choosing to believe the truth that *God is enough*, I remembered positive aspects of the interview.

1. President Hawkins was supportive and respectful.
2. He wanted a Women's Ministry Program at Western Seminary – on site
3. He believed part of that process was educating the husband/pastor to learn more about women's needs. Dr. Hawkins felt that could best happen through a woman.

4. Dr. Hawkins thought an eighteen-month women's program could be a full-time job for me. He said I was the person for the role—but to pray. They needed four to six weeks of work before I would have a firm position.

I would hear from him in two weeks. That was March 19.

Two weeks. *Yeah, right.*

—

I woke up full of anxiety.

Why couldn't I simply enjoy reading books and planting flowers?

Farmer's daughter did. *But Lord, you have never been satisfied allowing me to do just that and frankly, neither would I after a while.*

This would be a God-sized assignment.

Perhaps this was also the Death of a Vision time.

Refine me, Lord. Help me to get back to where I was after I met with Dr. Sweeney—knowing you opened this door, so you will bring it to pass.

I am not a "high D." DISC personality style reveals people who are high "D" (Dominance) are extroverts, outgoing and task oriented.[2] They are decisive, driven and demanding. They typically have high confidence and are comfortable taking risks. On two strategic fronts I have been told you had to be a "high D" to get anything done. It has been hard to overcome that because I see so many "high D's" doing things. But Lord, I know from scripture you used all sorts of people. I am sure Moses was not a "High D," but he obeyed (reluctantly) and look what you did through him. It really was not Moses, *it was you.* You just needed a body, ear, and mouthpiece.

Thank you, Lord, for reminding me about my first trip to Chattanooga. I realized those national leaders, Kay Arthur, Evelyn Christenson, and many others had different personalities. They simply believed you would do the impossible and they stepped out in faith. They obeyed and trusted you to do it. I came away with a new realization stamped on my heart, soul and written in my prayer notebook: "Lord, there is nothing I can't do, if you, Lord, are doing it in and through me!"

And for the first time I believed it.

I have wondered what the Ministry Wives Network International was all about. Why did you have me be part of that, sit in with those national leaders? I believed the connection was important for the future—perhaps the "future" is near.

Lord, please draw me so close that I hear your heartbeat and am concerned about what concerns you. Show me the direction you want this to go.

Jesus through his Holy Spirit wants me.

I took you. I chose you. I broke you, to be given.

Yes, even a farmer's daughter.

Thank you for leading me to Psalm 27. Today is March 27.

I remain confident of this: I will see the goodness
of the LORD in the land of the living. (v.13)

Just as you told me, Lord, this "new thing" would be
something I would love and enjoy.

Wait for the LORD; be strong and take heart and
wait for the LORD (v. 14).

*Thank you, Lord, for confirming this morning your direction
in opening the doors at Western Seminary. I continue praying
you will lead Dr. Sweeney and Dr. Hawkins in the same way
you lead me. Please make clear to each of us what your plan is
for me and for Western Seminary.*

—

Today is two weeks since Dr. Hawkins said he would
call me.

No call.

—

Virtue magazine called. They wanted my article on
"Moving Again," but only 350 words instead of 650. I finished
it by noon. Then Today's Christian Woman (TCW) said they
wanted the entire article, up to 1500 words.

I received a job description for Associate Editor for Luis
Palau. *Timing?* The Associate Editor position starts July first
and is temporary and half-time.

Again, Lord, I ask you to show me your perfect will.

—

Another day passed. No phone call.

I called Bonnie.

She said the ball was in Dr. Hawkins court. She would leave a message for him.

So again, Lord, everything seems to be swirling around. Thank you for being my rock and my shield.

Still waiting. Hoping. Praying.

—

President Hawkins called. It was 8:45 p.m.

He said they have been developing the budget and the money is not there for a Women's Ministry program yet. I asked about teaching the Women's Ministry classes and the student wives' classes. He said he would need to check with Dr. Sweeney. He did not think full-time would be in the budget. I asked about teaching for the Institute for Church Health (ICH) too. He said he has no one else like me who can teach Women's Ministry for ICH. But they were two weeks away from submitting a proposal for a grant, after which would take time to process.

He asked what other positions I was considering. I told him Luis Palau. Dr. Hawkins ended by saying before I take another job, come talk further about this proposal.

Days passed.

I wrote Dr. Hawkins a two-page-letter telling him I needed

clarification. I built a case for ministering to pastors' wives *now*. Since that was what I would be doing, wouldn't WS be the perfect place to do it?

Writing a letter was a release.

—

Attending Multnomah Bible School's Women's Ministry Conference raised my spirit. I was asked to be on the Wellspring Board. They were eager to start a ministry to Pastors' Wives. They said I was their answer to a two-year prayer!

Oh Lord, only you could have orchestrated this. The others on the Board were all leaders of a variety of ministries for women. Women attending Wellspring events were from multiple states. They loved networking and starting Wellspring in their areas. Several local events for pastors' wives were planned by the team. I would be ministering to pastors' wives!

Someone was saying it aloud! Pam Reeve's message at the conference: An Intimate Love Relationship with Jesus. *Lord, you affirmed again that you had given me this special message:* Fall in love with Jesus. I wept. Emotions surged.

Jesus wants me. *I am his.* I took you. I chose you. I broke you, all to be given.

—

Three weeks. Four. Five weeks passed.

Dr. Hawkins left a message to call his office on Monday to make an appointment for Tuesday. I was hopeful.

Until I called.

No one was in the office who could make an appointment for me. *Again?*

I called a friend for prayer. I walked with Lorraine. Then we picked up Jim from the airport. When I got home there was a phone message to meet Dr. Hawkins Tuesday at 2:30 in his office. *That's today!*

President Hawkins wanted me to develop their Women's Ministry program. He was offering me a full-time position: twenty-hours Women's Ministry, plus twenty-hours Advancement and Development Department. I met with the Department Head and his Assistant. I felt wonderfully comfortable and relaxed—lots of laughs and shared passions for ministry. I was there for two hours.

Then they said they would get back to me to confirm the offer.

Again?

Wait…wait…wait…

Is it really going to happen Lord?

—

The next day Vision Publishers offered me a job as Administrative Assistant. I would be giving support for the entire staff of ten.

I received a letter from Multnomah School of the Bible for a possible Adjunct Faculty position.

No word from Western Seminary. We were into the month of May.

A dear friend in charge of personnel for five counseling offices, again asked if I would consider a job administering the offices. She had asked me multiple times. She has been patient. She needed an answer. I finally told her I would give her an answer tomorrow by three o'clock.

If I did not hear from Western Seminary before three, I would take her job offer. I would assume WS could not make budget.

Tomorrow, Lord.

I will know. Won't I?

———

The next morning, I got a call to meet with President Hawkins at nine.

President Hawkins wanted me to start full-time work in a month, on June 1st!

What? Did he really say that?

Would you please repeat that, Dr. Hawkins?

"Yes, Bev. We believed from the start that you were the one God chose for this role. We worked hard to revise the budget. We now have an office ready for you in Armstrong Hall."

A farmer's daughter.

Lord, you have taken me from the farm, from the pasture ...
Like David.

> I (God) took you from the pasture and from
> tending the flock and appointed you ruler over
> my people...I have been with you wherever you
> have gone, and I have cut off all your enemies
> from before you. ... (I Chron 17:7-8).

God's dearly loved.

I took you. I chose you. I broke you, to be given.

Our greatest fulfillment is in giving ourselves to others.
Our gifts are the many ways in which we express who we are
as God's dearly loved.

Yes, even me.

A farmer's daughter.

Chapter 36

New Pastures

New pastures for this farmer's daughter

Is this really happening? On faculty and staff at Western Seminary?

My own office? Freedom to plan, to design, to bring together …

Design? Expand? *Yes!* Bring together.

The morning reading was 2 Chronicles 1.

> God told Solomon, "Ask for whatever you want
> me to give you." (v. 7)

Solomon asked for wisdom and knowledge to lead this people. And for one second, I felt a little envious. *Lord, I wish you would tell me the same thing.* Immediately he said, "What about the verses I gave you a few days ago and you wrote them in your prayer notebook."

I opened it up. There were two pages of Scriptures saying, "Whatever you ask in my name, I will do it." Typed verses. *Lord, I am so overjoyed!*

I asked you for wisdom, knowledge, and discernment for this new role.

I asked you then. I ask you now.

Jesus wants *me*. I am taken, chosen, broken, and now given!

Thank you, Lord, for preparing me in previous pastures.

And now.

New pastures

—

After only days in my new office President Hawkins asked if he could interview me on the radio. Western Seminary had a fifteen-minute daily radio program pre-recorded. An effective way to get the word out about new programs and courses for women, he said.

"Sure, Dr. Hawkins."

I spent more than fifteen minutes preparing questions and my answers for him to follow.

We walked into the studio. Two chairs were facing each other with the microphone inches from each other. I handed my questions to him.

He took them and quickly set them off to the side.

I became speechless. How would he know what to ask?

More important, how will I know what to answer?

"Good morning. Today we have with us… Bev, would you tell us something about yourself? How did you come to know Jesus? What brought you to Western? …"

W... h … a ... t ...?

I nearly froze. I did not expect this. Impromptu? *Me?*

Well, words did come out. I have no memory of what they were.

After fifteen minutes the program ended.

Then he said, "Now let's record a second program. Where are your questions, Bev?"

I was ready. And tried to relax.

After it was over and we both walked back to Armstrong Hall, he asked the question.

"Bev, how about you hosting the radio program every Friday? It could focus on women."

New pastures.

—

New pastures.

Unlimited. Innumerable. Never ending.

I was reminded of the time in South Florida when I was asked by Moody Bible Institute to be interviewed on the radio. *Scared!* First time for a few minutes over the phone. Later an hour in the studio. *Was that rehearsal for now?*

I also remembered the time when our kids went off the college and I was looking for a paying job. I went to Western Seminary. I felt sure God wanted me to check out the options there. Yet I could not understand why God would have sent me there only to be denied a job. Now I understood—seven years later. To prepare the way for the real thing.

God brought back to mind the first time I taught the last segment of a class Lyn Ludwig taught at Western Seminary, per her request. I was in a classroom at Western Seminary. I had this very intimidating experience before. Now it is more familiar. *God was preparing me.*

A teaching job at Western Seminary.

Me! A farmer's daughter.

—

I am starting to believe that a farmer's daughter can *be God's beloved.*

And I am.

But it is taking me a lifetime to learn to *live as God's beloved.*

I realized mentally I was *taken,* but I did not feel it or live it. *Chosen* took many years, evolving into being *broken.* Painful, yet the greatest gift of my life. It was then that I truly saw my deep need for more of Jesus. He met me there. *Broken.* And that led to God's eternal plan that *I be given.*

Then I could begin *living as God's beloved.*

Henri J. M. Nouwen in, *Life of the Beloved,* explains the journey.1 We *are* the beloved, yet spend a lifetime becoming the beloved, to live as the beloved. Our greatest fulfillment comes in giving ourselves to others. That is *living as the beloved.* Our gifts are the many ways in which we express who we are as God's beloved. Who can we be for each other?

It has taken me most of my life to learn this truth. And now to experience it.

—

The next morning, I awoke after an unusual dream.

I feel the need to have it interpreted because I knew it was from God.

I was swimming in the middle of the ocean by myself. Suddenly I looked up and there were humongous waves--fifty to sixty stories high--all around me. Waves ready to crash in on me and drown me.

There was seemingly no way to survive.

The winds increased. As I looked at the waves above me, I saw the sky above them and it was tumultuous—*dark, huge clouds* –very threatening! There was not time to think—it all seemed to happen in a split second. Almost immediately, after seeing the impending danger, I was catapulted up out of the water above the waves and sent flying to the shore in safety.

I woke up before I landed. As I was catapulted into the air, I knew it was God supernaturally rescuing me from a sure death. It all seemed to happen in a micro-second. Immediately I felt peace—and incredible confidence and joy in the Lord's deliverance.

I went to the Psalm for that day (18th of the month). It was Psalm 18.

> He reached down from on high and took hold of me.
>
> He drew me out of deep waters. ...
>
> The LORD was my support. He brought me out into a spacious place. He rescued me because he delighted in me. (v. 16, 18b, 19)

What? So hard to grasp... the battle ... the enemy ... Goliath. These verses ... trying to catch my breath. *Rescued.* Just minutes after the dream. The visual. The emotional experience. The truth. The purpose. God's message to *me!*

He rescued me because he delighted in me? Repeat. He delighted in me. Jesus delighted in *me.* Repeat. *Jesus rescued me* because Jesus delights in me!

God has chosen me! I am God's beloved!

No longer "Ordinary me."

Intimacy with Jesus. That is my heart's deepest desire.

"I want to hear your voice, Lord. I want to see your perspective, your direction, and receive your empowerment. Like David, you pulled me from tending sheep where no one noticed, to the big city of Portland, Oregon. I walked into Western Seminary *only* in obedience to you, Lord. It was like David agreeing to leave the sheep and come to Samuel's anointing. He obeyed. He could have chosen not to."

Jesus has given only you the power of choice for you. *I choose Jesus.*

I obeyed, Lord, and it seems you have given me the dream of a lifetime job. Like David, you knew this was your plan for me the day I was born, and I must assume you have prepared me for this. I feel I have so much to learn—*and I do!*

I know you, Lord, are powerful enough to conquer the Goliaths in my life. Everyday.

The lies: we don't want you; we would be better off without you; we want you to meet our expectations. I never had a choice. I am not enough.

My daily prayer:

Lord, give me the ability to discern lies and reject them.

Lord, give me the ability to discern your truths and embrace them.

Jesus says:

I want you. You are chosen.

You are better with me/Jesus.

I/Jesus will speak to your expectations.

I/Jesus brings real/full joy.

Jesus is enough.

I want to feel your unconditional love and reassurance that

I am walking in your way and that you are there alongside me. *Always.*

This farmer's daughter does not *ever* want to leave this new pasture.

Chapter 37

Green Pastures

Twenty years of unimaginable green pastures followed.

The making of a shepherd, *me*.

The experiences God had taken me through all my life prepared me for these green pastures. I began to understand better why he took me from the ends of the earth, chose me, yet broke me, to give me. And promised to strengthen me, help me, hold me with His right hand. I needed God every step of the way. He went before me and behind me. My shepherd was training me to become a shepherd too. I remember those words spoken by my colleagues at my retirement.

"Shepherd the flock of God among you" (I Peter 5:2) NASB

New visions, new plans, innovative programs, new courses, new students, new leaders at Western Seminary in Portland, Oregon and beyond. Accepted, embraced, and encouraged by my faculty colleagues, Dr. Jim Sweeney, Dean of Faculty, and President Randy Roberts.

Yes, the Lord opened the door for me to work full-time to develop a Women's Center for Ministry at Western Seminary. This involved regular events to encourage and enhance leadership in ministry. These events were open to any woman wanting to gain more insight and experience in ministry—on multiple levels. It became a global hub for training, resources, and networking for women in ministry.

Many women involved in church ministries were married to pastors, as was I. This opened the door to develop a Pastor's Wives Advisory Board, a team to plan gatherings just for wives of men in full-time ministries.

Another step was developing a Women's Ministry specialization for the Master's Degree and Doctor of Ministry programs. God led me to design and teach multiple courses, both at our Portland, San Jose, and Sacramento campuses. Pastoral Care for Women, credit and non-credit courses, weekend, and week-long classes.

I could not have moved forward if God had not provided Kenine Stein as an Administrative Assistant. She was essential in each step taken in these green pastures. She prayed. She worked. She prayed. She understood. She prayed. She gave me insight, discernment, and joy. She blessed me every day. I am eternally grateful for her. *Thank you, Kenine.*

After reading a stack of books and requiring students to read them, God led me to write two books: *Shepherding A Woman's Heart: A New Model for Effective Ministry Women*; and *Shepherding Women in Pain: Real Women, Real Issues, and What You Need to Know to Truly Help.* Both were published by Moody Publishers and used in their schools as well as WS. These resources were filled with lessons I learned in shepherding women, plus instructions from multiple shepherds.

At one of the national women's conferences in Texas, while I was standing at the WS Women's Ministry display table between sessions, a woman came up and asked if I had a Doctor of Ministry degree.

"Well, no, I don't. I have a Master's degree. Why do you ask?"

"Would you like one?" Alice Mathews walked me to her display table from Gordon-Conwell Theological Seminary in South Hamilton, Massachusetts.

What? I live in Oregon. I have a more-than-full-time job.

What a surprise to learn she was leading a program for women just like me. Two weeks each summer on GCTS campus, followed by required work done back home throughout the year. The program was designed and filled with women from across the U.S., with a desire to provide more training for women in ministry, like me. We enjoyed great collaborations and insights each time we met.

A Doctor of Ministry degree. Me? Yes! What a sovereign act of God. That huge credential on my wall includes the signature of Billy Graham, the co-founder of GCTS. What a gift. I learned so much during those years. That experience and the credential enhanced the ministry God gave me at WS and beyond. I am eternally grateful!

Dr. Bev Hislop, Professor of Pastoral Care. *Me?* Ordinary me?

Farmer's daughter. No more peeking through the cracks.

Traveling through and beyond the cracks. Out into the green pastures!

The LORD is my shepherd, I lack nothing. He makes me lie down in green pastures. (Psalm 23:1-2a)

The righteous will flourish like a palm tree... they will flourish...they will still bear fruit in old age, they will stay fresh and green, proclaiming, 'The LORD is upright; he is my Rock...' (Psalm 92:12 -15)

The LORD will guide you always, he will satisfy your needs in a sun scorched land and will strengthen your frame. You will be like a well-watered garden, like a spring who waters never fail. (Isaiah 58:11)

As we end this journey together, I leave these verses with you. These truths carry me every day and I trust they will you.

"Let all who are wise heed these things and ponder the loving deeds of the LORD." (Psalm 107:43)

Appendices

LIES	TRUTH
We don't want you.	JESUS wants me.
	I am God's dearly loved
	I Took You
	Isaiah 41:9
We would be better off without you.	I am better with JESUS.
	I am God's dearly loved
	I Chose You
	Isaiah 41:9
We want you to meet our expectations	JESUS speaks to expectations.
	I am God's dearly loved ·
	I Broke You
	Isaiah 41:10; John 15:16
Don't anticipate joy or fun, you will be disappointed every time.	JESUS brings full joy.
	I am God's dearly loved.
	To Be Given
	Isaiah 41:10; John 15:9-11

You are not enough	JESUS is enough.
	I am God's dearly loved.
	Living as God's dearly loved
	2 Cor. 12:9, 10c

Lies I Believed vs. Truths God Says

Isaiah 41:9-10

We don't want you.

"I have chosen you" (TNIV)

"You are my chosen..." (CEV)

"You're my first choice." (MSG)

We would be better off without you.

"I took you from the ends of the earth. I called you. I said, 'you are my servant.'" (TNIV)

"From far across the earth, I brought you here and said, 'You are my chosen servant." (CEV)

"I pulled you in from all over the world, called you in from every dark corner of the earth, telling you, 'You're my servant, serving at my side." (MSG)

We want you to meet our expectations.

"I am with you, so do not fear." (TNIV)

"I am with you, so don't be afraid." (CEV)

"I picked you; I haven't dropped you. Don't panic. I'm with you." (MSG)

Don't anticipate joy or fun, you will be disappointed every time.

> "I am your God, do not be dismayed" (TNIV)
>
> "I am your God. I will make you strong." (CEV)
>
> "There is no need to fear for I'm your God." (MSG)

You are not enough.

> "I will strengthen you and help you. I will uphold you with my righteous right hand." (TNIV)
>
> "I will make you strong, as I protect you with my arm and give you victories." (CEV)
>
> "I'll give you strength. I'll help you. I'll hold you steady, keep a firm grip on you." (MSG)

The LORD your God is with you

He is mighty to save

He will take great delight in you

He will quiet you with his love

He will rejoice over you with singing.

(Zephaniah 3:17) NIV

—

"I will sing of the LORD's great love forever; with my mouth I will make your faithfulness known through all generations. I will declare that your love stands firm forever, that you have established your faithfulness in heaven itself." (Psalm 89:1-2)

—

"Those who are wise will take all this to heart;

they will see in our history the
faithful love of the LORD.

(Psalm 107:43) NLT

Acknowledgments

As this memoir unfolds, you will see an endless number of people who have contributed to my life journey. My life-long journal stored their names and details of each impactful moment. Some are named, others are not. There are too many to name in this setting. Please know *I am so, so grateful to each of you!*

I am especially thankful for the daily patience, grace, honesty, and forgiveness of my family. My parents, Connie and Ray White; my siblings, Paul, Palmer, and Carole.

Our married children, Lorraine (and Gene) and Dan (and Maureen) continue to be such a joy, along with their children, Madeline, Katie, Emma, Hannah, Zach, and Matthew. *You all have blessed me beyond words.*

My dearest husband, Jim has led the way for this incredibly challenging and blessed journey together. *I cannot thank you enough, dear. You are an incredible gift to me and to the world!*

Notes

Chapter 1: The Cracks

1. Huntington's disease is a condition that affects the brain and gets worse over time. Symptoms, such as movements you can't control, usually start between the ages of 30 and 50. Sometimes symptoms appear earlier in children who have juvenile HD. The disease is passed down through family genes, which determine your physical characteristics. But the main factor is whether you have a parent with HD. If you do, you have a 50% chance of also having the disease.

https://my.clevelandclinic.org/health/diseases/14369-huntingtons-disease

Chorea, which is sometimes a symptom of Huntington's disease, but not deadly, is one of several known involuntary movements, which also include more common ones such as tremor and tics. To the untrained eye, it can be challenging to identify chorea, because its appearance varies from one individual to another. Over time, it became known as "Huntington's chorea" but because not everyone who suffers from the condition experiences chorea, the name was changed to "Huntington's disease." And in its advanced stages, a person can die from complications from it. While there is no cure, there's an increasing amount of research devoted to finding one. https://www.stonybrookmedicine.edu/patientcare/askexpert/huntingtons/chorea/schwartz

Chapter 11: Over and Out

1. Stage 1 is PROTEST. Disoriented, numb. Nothing is wrong, I am fine.

Stage 2 is DESPAIR. Confused, fear, sadness—the gamut of emotions. Our thinking ability is severely limited. "I know I can't make it."

Stage 3 is DETACHMENT. Emptiness, deadness, and numbness. Yet, we realize we must adjust to the new environment in which the loss exists.

Stage 4 is RECOVERY. Positive thoughts enter. We begin investing energy into the new. This stage takes longer.

Stage 5 is RESTORATION. Hope returns and reconstruction increases self-confidence. Thinking is clearer. We will take initiative for progress and reattachments.

Shepherding Women in Pain, Bev Hislop (Moody Publishers, 2020), 39-42.

Chapter 17: The Landline Rings

1. Actual lyrics from original 1979 Imperial version
https://www.letssingit.com/the-imperials-lyrics-he-didn-t-lift-us-up-to-let-us-down-pp1f6m2

2. Imperials singing this song, https://www.youtube.com/watch?v=_OU5A7RSRYc

Chapter 20: I Don't Have Time Now

1. *Hurt People, Hurt People*, by Sandra D. Wilson, (Thomas Nelson Publishers, 1993).

Chapter 27: Welcome Home, Finally

1. As the Deer, song by the Maranatha! Singers

Copyright: 1984 Universal Music – Brentwood Benson Publishing Songwriter: Martin J. Nystrom; As the Deer lyrics © Capitol Christian Music Group, Capitol CMG Publishing, Warner Chappell Music, Inc

2. In Moments Like These, song by The Maranatha! Singers. Songwriter: David Graham © 1980 C. A. Music (a div. of C.A. Records).

Chapter 30: You Didn't Bring Us This Far

1. Actual lyrics from original 1979 Imperial version https://www.letssingit.com/the-imperials-lyrics-h e-didn-t-lift-us-up-to-let-us-down-pp1f6m2

2. Ibid.

3. Ibid.

4. Henry T. Blackaby and Claude V. King, *Experiencing God, Knowing and Doing the Will of God workbook* (Lifeway Press, 1990), 73 – 75.

Chapter 31: Startled

1. https://www.psychologytoday.com/us/basics/burnout

2. Bill Thrall, Bruce McNicol, and Ken McElrath, *The Ascent of a Leader* (Jossey-Bass, first edition, 1999), 81.

Chapter 35: Farmer's Daughter

1. Henry T. Blackaby and Claude V. King, *Experiencing God, Knowing and Doing the Will of God* (Lifeway Press, 1990), 142.

2. https://www.discprofile.com/what-is-disc/disc-styles

Chapter 36: New Pastures

1. Henri J.M. Nouwen, *Life of the Beloved,* (Crossroad Publishing Company, 1992), Contents.

About the Author

Bev Hislop (D. Min., Gordon-Cornwell Theological Seminary) has served as Professor of Pastoral Care to Women and the Executive Director of the Women's Center for Ministry at Western Seminary in Portland, Oregon. She also taught at Western's San Jose and Sacramento campuses. She served on the board of Network of Women in Leadership and was the former host of the weekly radio program *Western Connection for Women*. Bev has authored S*hepherding a Woman's Heart: A New Model for Effective Ministry to Women*, and *Shepherding Women in Pain: Real Women, Real Issues, and What You Need to Know to Truly Help*, both by Moody Publishers. Bev and her husband, Jim, have two married children and six grandchildren.

Printed in the United States
by Baker & Taylor Publisher Services